Gold

Resources series

Michael Bradshaw and Tim Boersma, *Natural Gas*
Gavin Bridge and Philippe Le Billon, *Oil*, 2nd edition
Anthony Burke, *Uranium*
Jennifer Clapp, *Food*, 3rd edition
Peter Dauvergne and Jane Lister, *Timber*
Elizabeth R. DeSombre and J. Samuel Barkin, *Fish*
Kate Ervine, *Carbon*
David Lewis Feldman, *Water*
Gavin Fridell, *Coffee*
Derek Hall, *Land*
Andrew Herod, *Labor*
Kristy Leissle, *Cocoa*
Michael Nest, *Coltan*
Kate O'Neill, *Waste*
Bronwyn Parry and Beth Greenhough, *Bioinformation*
Ben Richardson, *Sugar*
Ian Smillie, *Diamonds*
Adam Sneyd, *Cotton*
Bill Winders, *Grains*

Gold

MICHAEL JOHN BLOOMFIELD AND
ROY MACONACHIE

polity

First published in 2021 by Polity Press

Polity Press
65 Bridge Street
Cambridge CB2 1UR, UK

Polity Press
101 Station Landing
Suite 300
Medford, MA 02155, USA

ISBN-13: 978-1-5095-3410-4
ISBN-13: 978-1-5095-3411-1 (pb)

A catalogue record for this book is available from the British Library.

Library of Congress Cataloging-in-Publication Data

Names: Bloomfield, Michael John, author. | Maconachie, Roy, author.
Title: Gold / Michael Bloomfield and Roy Maconachie.
Description: Cambridge, UK ; Medford, MA : Polity Press, 2020. | Series:
  Resources | Includes bibliographical references and index. | Summary:
  "Pithy introduction to the geopolitics of the world's most coveted
  asset"-- Provided by publisher.
Identifiers: LCCN 2020020747 (print) | LCCN 2020020748 (ebook) | ISBN
  9781509534104 (hardback) | ISBN 9781509534111 (paperback) | ISBN
  9781509534128 (epub)
Subjects: LCSH: Gold industry. | Gold mines and mining.
Classification: LCC HD9536.A2 B56 2020 (print) | LCC HD9536.A2 (ebook) |
  DDC 338.2/741--dc23
LC record available at https://lccn.loc.gov/2020020747
LC ebook record available at https://lccn.loc.gov/2020020748

Typeset in 11 on 14 pt Sabon by
Servis Filmsetting Ltd, Stockport, Cheshire
Printed and bound in Great Britain by CPI Group (UK) Ltd, Croydon

The publisher has used its best endeavours to ensure that the URLs for external websites referred to in this book are correct and active at the time of going to press. However, the publisher has no responsibility for the websites and can make no guarantee that a site will remain live or that the content is or will remain appropriate.

For further information on Polity, visit our website:
politybooks.com

Contents

Illustrations   vi
Acknowledgements   viii
Abbreviations   x

1   Introduction   1

2   Gold and the Distortions of Development   13

3   An Intractable Industry   45

4   Gold Governance and Gaps   78

5   Rising Powers in Supply and Demand   112

6   Conclusion: Refocusing for the Future of Gold   141

    Notes   153
    Selected Readings   179
    Index   185

Illustrations

Figures

3.1 Distribution of gold reserves worldwide by
    country, 2019 53
3.2 Global mine production of top ten countries, 2018 53
3.3 Top ten gold mining companies, 2018 55
3.4 Gold jewellery supply chain 63
3.5 The gold supply chain 65
4.1 No Dirty Gold ad campaign from *The New York*
    Times 88
4.2 The No Dirty Gold strategy 90
4.3 The six steps of the DRC's conflict-gold supply
    chain 102
5.1 GDP growth per capita 120
5.2 Official gold holdings of top ten countries, 2019 125
5.3 Foreign reserves held in gold of top ten countries,
    2019 (%) 126

Tables

3.1 Leading mining companies worldwide based on
    market capitalisation, 2019 54
4.1 The World Gold Council's Conflict-Free Gold
    Standard 99

Boxes

4.1 The No Dirty Gold campaign's 'Golden Rules'   89
4.2 Key objectives for Fairtrade mining organisations 95

Acknowledgements

Many people have been involved in this project, both directly and indirectly. We are grateful to all of those individuals who have contributed to discussions on gold and shaped our thinking over the years. They are too numerous to name, but they include many of the people and organisations mentioned in the book. They have provided both expertise and insights into this unique industry, and we have tried to accurately reflect their sometimes competing perspectives throughout.

We would also like to thank our colleagues at the University of Bath, especially those in the Centre for Development Studies, the Department of Social and Policy Sciences, and the Centre for Business, Organisations and Society. But our colleagues and collaborators are based across institutions, and so we would be remiss not to mention the support we've received from friends at IDS Sussex, Queen Elizabeth House at the University of Oxford, SPERI at the University of Sheffield, the University of Surrey, the University of London (especially the LSE and affiliates gang), the University of British Columbia, Clark University, and the Earth System Governance Project at the University of Utrecht.

Michael would like to thank Peter Klein and Jane Lister, as well as the entire Hidden Costs of Global Supply Chains team, located at UBC and partner institutions across the world. The project is an exciting collaboration between journalists and academics funded by the Social Science and Humanities Research

Council of Canada. Among its members are many contributors to the Polity Press Resources Series, including Jennifer Clapp, Peter Dauvergne, Gavin Fridell, Philippe Le Billon and Jane Lister, and it has helped support the research that has gone into this book. Some recent collaborators that have also assisted in shaping his thinking on the regulation of global commodities, and so deserve special mention, are James Copestake, Andrew Crane, Genevieve LeBaron, Nivi Manchanda, Philip Schleifer, Vivek Soundararajan, Laura Spence and Yixian Sun.

Roy would like to express his sincere gratitude to numerous colleagues in West Africa who, over many years, have shared their knowledge and experiences on gold mining, among whom are Sahr Mani, Felix Conteh, Solomon Gbanie, Kabba Bangura, Daniel Gbondo and Stephen 'Atta' Okyere.

We would also like to thank Patrick Loughran for his invaluable editorial assistance and Namita Shete for her tremendous research assistance. Needless to say, a huge thank you goes to Louise Knight, Inès Boxman, and the entire team at Polity for their support and patience, as well as to the anonymous reviewers for their insightful comments.

Most of all, we would like to thank our families for their support and kindness and for the time they allowed us to complete this project. Michael would like to thank his family and friends, but none more so than Sarah, who endured and enjoyed many evenings of peace and quiet as writing progressed. Roy would like to thank Elizabeth, Max, Edie and Jonas for all of their love and patience.

Abbreviations

ASGM	artisanal small-scale gold mining
BRICS	Brazil, Russia, India, China and South Africa
CDA	community development agreement
CNGGC	China National Gold Group Corporation
CSR	corporate social responsibility
DRC	Democratic Republic of Congo
EIR	extractive industries review
ESIA	environmental and social impact assessment
FDI	foreign direct investment
GDP	gross domestic product
GFC	global financial crisis
ISEAL	International Social and Environmental Accreditation and Labelling Alliance
LSGM	large-scale gold mining
MDF	Minerals Development Fund
NFC	near-field communication
NGO	non-governmental organisation
OECD	Organisation for Economic Co-operation and Development
OTC	over the counter
PAMP	Produits Artistiques Métaux Précieux
QR	quick response
RBA	Responsible Business Alliance
RFID	radio-frequency identification
RJC	Responsible Jewellery Council

SDG   Sustainable Development Goal
SGE   Shanghai Gold Exchange
SHFE Shanghai Futures Exchange
TSX   Toronto Stock Exchange
UAE   United Arab Emirates
UNDP United Nations Development Programme
UNSC United Nations Security Council
WGC   World Gold Council

CHAPTER I

Introduction

The year is 1979, and deep in the Amazon rainforest of Brazil an ominous discovery is about to be made. A local boy, playing in a swimming hole, spots a shiny object in the mud. Washing it clean with the clear, jungle water, even such a young boy knows this small golden nugget is a special discovery. He sprints off to tell the adults.

The boy works on the struggling farm of landowner Genesio Ferreira da Silva. When Genesio learns of the discovery, he feels he has been blessed, and his troubles may finally be over. The landowner hires a geologist, who comes out to the jungle and confirms what Genesio had scarcely allowed himself to hope: there is much more gold to be found here. Neither the geologist nor the landowner could have known this would soon become the site of the infamous Serra Pelada mine, one of the largest gold mines in the Amazon.

It didn't take long for word to spread through the jungle. Prospectors, seeking their fortune, came by the dozen, then the hundreds, then the thousands. At first, Genesio made money from the find. He leased a strip of his land to a local business-man, who built an airfield to access the mine, and Genesio charged for its use. But soon the enormity of the deposit became clear: this was a major discovery of gold. Word spread far beyond the jungle, to the centres of power in Rio, São Paulo and Brasília. The ruling military dictatorship sniffed oppor-tunity. The army swooped in and took over operations. The powerful came to claim the riches, while local people were sidelined and exploited.

Still, a few of the principles upon which Genesio founded the site remained. In what was quickly becoming a stinking and muddy wasteland, alcohol was forbidden, as was prostitution. In the middle of this impromptu settlement – what many referred to as 'Babylonia', in reference to the scale of excavation and slave-labour-like conditions – was a square where miners gathered to swap stories of gold and women. This part of town came to be known as the 'Square of Lies', befitting of the tall tales that seem to accompany prospectors and mine sites around the world and throughout time. Life was hard for the miners, and only a lucky few made their fortune.[1]

The story of Genesio Ferreira da Silva and the Serra Pelada mine is a stark but familiar tale of how the discovery of gold can begin as a blessing, but can all too easily spiral into injustice and depravity. As often as not, a gold find turns out to be an excavation of disappointment, destruction and general misery. This true story sounds a bit like a modern-day fable, nicely illustrating some of the ways in which gold is truly a unique commodity: in its promise, in its impacts, in its links to power and, perhaps implicitly, in the challenges it poses for those who seek to govern it.

The argument we make in this book is straightforward: gold is uniquely impactful on the lives of people and the planet. It is also uniquely difficult to regulate. This is because of its historical importance in centres of geopolitical and financial power, its deep cultural resonance across time and space, its physical characteristics and the complexity of its supply and demand, and the culture that continues to permeate the industry itself.

There has been no shortage of new and exciting regulatory initiatives emerging that aim to mitigate some of the worst social and environmental issues driven by gold production and consumption. But, despite these often valiant efforts, and despite popular claims to the contrary, these initiatives have so far fallen short of making gold a force for good. And the situation only appears to be getting worse. Changes in the gold industry, driven by power shifts at the highest levels of the global political economy, are making gold supply chains even more difficult to govern.

In this book, we aim to explain why this is the case. Why is gold uniquely impactful and, relatedly, why is gold so difficult to regulate? Why are current efforts to regulate gold falling short and why will efforts to govern gold likely become even more difficult in the future? And, perhaps even more importantly, what can we do about it? While we do not profess to hold all the answers, we offer our informed perspective on what has gone wrong, while also suggesting how we might refocus our attention on areas in which real progress could be made.

Gold's continuing relevance

For some, gold rushes might seem like an occurrence of the past. Compared to other resources, gold might even seem to be a bit old fashioned. After all, the gold standard is long obsolete, and financial markets seem preoccupied with abstract derivatives or energy commodities such as oil. Yet gold is still highly sought after, and gold rushes still occur with regularity. If anything, the story of gold is more important to the global economy now than ever before. It is a commodity with high liquidity. It can be smuggled. It is traded for political favours. It is the embodiment of power. The Amazonian Gold Rush of which Genesio Ferreira da Silva unwittingly became the centre took place in the 1980s. Yet now history is repeating, as a new gold rush gains momentum in the jungle.

Gold mining had gone relatively quiet in the Amazon until prices spiked in response to the global financial crisis of 2007–8. Now, once again, the sounds of chainsaws and earthmovers startle macaws from their trees. This modern-day gold rush rivals those in nineteenth-century California and the Klondike in the fervour it has stirred and the fortune seekers it has attracted. It is also widespread throughout the Amazon region, spanning several countries. And, like the gold rushes of old, it isn't well regulated.

In Colombia, for example, the government admits that profits from illegal mining far outstrip those from drug trafficking – perhaps as much as three times over – with much of the money funding various criminal organisations and guerrilla groups.[2] It has sparked ecological destruction on a global scale and is a human rights catastrophe that is being compared to that associated with African 'blood diamonds'. Credible allegations of sex trafficking and child labour abound.[3] The Colombian Amazon has always been popular with drug kingpins, but now they are laundering billions of dollars through gold mining, diversifying their coca business.[4]

After passing through many middlemen along the way, Colombian gold has been smuggled to huge refiners, including NTR Metals in the United States. Reports indicate that NTR seemed to have supplied the refined metal to major brands, ranging from Apple (for electronic parts) to Tiffany & Co. (for jewellery), before the companies cut ties when word got out about the refiner's dodgy practices. This eventually led to criminal charges for three gold dealers working for NTR Metals.

Breakaway factions of the country's guerrilla movements, FARC and the National Liberation Army (or ELN), are active in this part of the Colombian jungle, and across the border in Venezuela as well. These groups have been blamed for the murders of miners on the border. Neither the gold nor the trouble stays long in the jungle. They permeate porous borders and infiltrate both national and international politics and the highest echelons of power in the global political economy.

In Caracas, the government has been cashing in on the gold rush. With oil production floundering and US sanctions taking hold, President Nicolas Maduro's government has turned to gold to ease the pressures of crippling debt amid limited options.[5] The US and its allies have wanted Maduro ousted from power for some time, and they have imposed economic sanctions on both oil and gold to put pressure on his government. But gold remains relatively easy to smuggle and to sell. In 2018, Turkey purchased mass quantities of Venezuelan gold, to the tune of 20 metric tonnes, or about US$1 billion worth.[6] Turkey has been buying significant quantities of gold lately and has not appeared worried about US sanctions. In fact, according to Suzanne Maloney, senior fellow and deputy director of foreign policy at the Brookings Institution, Turkey has long used its gold to buy Iranian oil in circumvention of US sanctions.[7] And she believes Turkey will do the same with Venezuelan gold.[8]

While this particular situation is clearly still evolving, these events are rather telling in terms of defining gold's role in politics and the economy. Gold continues to change lives and landscapes wherever it is found, while trickling like a bright, bitter seam through the world's geopolitical and financial centres. This book is the story of gold today. From the half a billion dollar open pit mine soon to commence operation in Siberia, to the insatiable demand for gold in the electronic devices that permeate our daily lives, or the environmental desolation driven by gold mining in the Amazon that threatens the stability of Earth's ecosystems, this is a story we overlook at our peril.

Gold's continuing allure

One of the curious things about gold, unlike many other geo-politically significant resources such as oil, is that it is fairly evenly distributed geographically around the world. Although it is mined on every continent, gold remains extremely scarce, which adds to its value. But why is it so valuable in the first place?

Gold holds monetary value and is extremely fungible. But, in contrast to paper money or electronic currency, gold has high inherent value as a material. Its many uses include jewellery of course. It is naturally beautiful and has been the precious metal of choice for artefacts and adornment fashioned in almost every civilisation. The shiny metal has never lost its fascination for us, and this is probably its most visible and familiar manifestation. But gold has many practical uses. It is highly malleable, making it suitable for moulding anything, including jewellery but also dental products. Gold is also a superb conductor, and so remains an essential input sought after by the electronics industry. In fact, it is perhaps thanks to this industry that most people's relationship to gold might be closer than it first appears.

For example, the average person in the developed world will hold gold in their hands for about four hours per day. That's how long we spend on our smartphones daily, and every smartphone contains gold. The precious metal is an excellent conductor. Faster than copper, and more durable than silver, it is a key component in laptops, tablets and PCs. Gold permeates our lives. It links us, economically and ethically, to the people who mine it, manufacture it and trade it. From the miner working with shovel and pickaxe in the Democratic Republic of Congo, to the assembly line worker soldering circuit boards in China, to the hedge fund manager in a tailored suit trading gold futures in London, to the consumer on the high street, the lifecycle of gold today is truly global.

But it isn't only the physical nature of the metal that makes it such a fascinating resource. It is the symbolism we have attached to it. As the Amazon vignette clearly illustrates, throughout history, gold has been associated with power, prestige and promise. The powerful have sought it out, sometimes through market exchange and at other times through conquest and conflict. Indeed, governments still hoard vast amounts of it. Wealth in gold is perhaps the closest we come to a physical manifestation of power; it is power in fungible form. It represents both stability and opportunity, and this symbolism is near universal.

Gold does not corrode or tarnish easily, and perhaps it is this enduring quality that also imbues it with symbolism for us. It suggests timelessness. No wonder the phonograph records on NASA's space probes Voyager spacecraft 1 and 2 are made of gold. The two records contain sounds and images of life and culture on planet Earth. And, as the two NASA vessels journey beyond our solar system into interstellar space, the gold will endure, longer than we shall.

There are many reasons people want to own gold, whether in bars, coins or jewellery. Beyond its beauty, gold has deep cultural and religious significance. Gold is gifted the world over, at weddings, graduations and other special events. The social exchange of gold comes with status. But, again, it also represents stability. In India, for example, banks accept gold jewellery as collateral, and families borrow against this when times demand it. Nowadays, in many societies, the promise gold represents is most clearly demonstrated when it comes in the form of an engagement ring.

Gold, of course, offers promise when it is still in the ground. And such promise has sparked major 'gold rushes' on just about every continent, from the Amazon to sub-Saharan Africa, from the Klondike to the Siberian steppe. Gold holds this same promise today in countries around the world, especially poorer nations struggling to develop their economies. Here, the discovery of gold is intertwined with the discovery of possibility – the possibility to develop autonomously, free from neo-colonial oppression and poverty. But the truth is, and as Genesio and countless others have learned, that the poor rarely become rich, and the powerless often remain marginalised. Yes, gold has a dark side. Despite the promise of gold, why do the profits of gold extraction rarely benefit the poor? How can we harness the power of gold in ways that promote more equitable outcomes instead of reinscribing existing inequalities, as is too often the case? And whose responsibility is it?

Many activist groups – from Earthworks, to Oxfam, to Human Rights Watch, to the Enough Project – have attempted to strengthen the link between consumers of gold and the practices that produce it. From their perspective, each of us is implicated in the conflicts that gold fuels and the pollution of groundwater that gold mining causes. We become caught up in the corruption lubricating the advancement of industrial-scale projects, which funnels money into the hands of the few, to the detriment of the many. When we buy gold – in our phones, laptops and wedding rings, and even through our pension funds – we play a role in adding to the development challenges (and potential opportunities) of resource-rich but often impoverished countries. Thus do we, as consumers, also assume a role in perpetuating conflict in nations or regions where instability is a near constant feature? If we accept this link, then we also acknowledge that each of us also has a potential role to play in the governance of gold, helping to ensure the worst impacts of gold mining are mitigated while the best outcomes are amplified.

Outline of the book

Throughout the rest of the book, we take you on a journey along the global gold supply chain, revealing the practice of producing gold, the people who drive it, and the harms and benefits that accompany the unearthing and consolidation of this intoxicating resource. Below, we outline the path we take, with each chapter covering a step in the central argument: that gold produces social, economic and environmental impacts like no other metal but at the same time remains extremely difficult to regulate, which is largely why current efforts have fallen short. Regulating gold appears to be getting more difficult given global shifts in production and consumption, but there are some areas on which we can focus to promote real, positive change.

In chapter 2, we investigate the ways in which gold affects people's lives and the life of the planet. From the impacts of scrambles to obtain it to the colonial holdover of extractive and enclave economies, gold production and consumption continue to reflect and reinforce power discrepancies within and across societies. Historically, the supply and demand for gold has been closely connected to geopolitical shifts and financial events taking place at the commanding heights of the global economy. Linked to the most powerful in society, the quest for gold has too often superseded any social or ecological concerns. In the chapter, we reflect on this history and offer brief overviews of some of the main contemporary concerns related to gold production, including issues associated with the so-called resource curse, disputes around unequal revenue sharing, the ecological impacts of gold mining, and the links between gold and conflict. Historically, all things considered, there are very few resources that have shaped economies and societies to the same degree as gold.

Chapter 3 argues that many of these issues persist because gold remains an exceedingly difficult resource to regulate. This is not only because of its entrenched links to centres of power but also because of (1) its material characteristics and the complexity of its supply chains and (2) the related lack of transparency and 'cowboy culture' that permeate the industry. Gold's physical characteristics, including its ability to be melted and recycled, add complexity to a supply chain that includes many players, multiple forms and myriad uses. All of this makes gold incredibly difficult to track and trace, complicating attempts to establish provenance of the resource and accountability of the users. And the culture of the industry itself – what we have come to call the 'cowboy culture' – has been built on stories of swashbuckling explorers, rogue traders and prospectors hoping to strike it rich. While the majority of actors in the global gold supply chain are above board, a culture of secrecy, distrust and corruption lingers under the surface and contributes to the difficulties in regulating this much sought-after substance.

In chapter 4, we evaluate the many innovative regulatory initiatives that have been created to govern gold. Even here, power plays a critical role in explaining how regulations are designed and which get taken up. Overall, our analysis concludes that attempts to regulate gold have thus far fallen short of achieving a truly responsible industry. While pockets of success are evident, there is much left to be desired, even if most of the actors involved in these initiatives have incentives to claim otherwise. The chapter introduces these regulatory actors, including the state governments where gold is extracted and those where trading takes place. It also includes activists, both in local and in transnational networks. The chapter outlines how a combination of state intransigence and activist pressure has led to powerful responses from the private sector, from civil society and from third-party states. We outline and evaluate these initiatives that span the spectrum of regulatory efforts, from corporate social responsibility (CSR), to certifications, to Fairtrade labels, to disclosure regulation in the form of the Dodd–Frank Act. In assessing the many challenges and innovations in the governance of gold, we conclude that there have been some successes but not enough truly to transform the industry into one in which responsibility is a core concern and an auditable outcome.

In chapter 5, we consider how recent and ongoing global shifts in the industry suggest that it is only going to become more difficult to regulate gold in the future. Gold is progressively becoming even more 'financialised', as new gold-backed trading instruments are developed to supply the seemingly insatiable demand for gold as a financial asset. The economic success of the so-called BRICS emerging economies has created a nascent middle class that is further swelling the market for these financial assets, as well as for gold in its physical form. But it is not just citizens flocking to the yellow metal. Governments from across the world are buying up and increasingly trading in gold, while large companies producing and dealing in gold are being created and are changing hands at a rapid pace. Perhaps the most consistent trend is that the centre of the global gold market is clearly shifting to the East. Combined, these developing trends have enormous and under-examined implications for the governance of gold. We evaluate the extent to which current strategies to create responsible gold will be up to the task.

Finally, chapter 6 concludes the book by focusing on possibilities to make gold work better for all stakeholders. While we do not pretend to have all the answers, we offer a perspective on the way forward for all the millions, in fact, billions of individuals who produce and consume gold. The chapter takes stock of the regulatory challenges we have outlined throughout, including how current efforts to produce 'responsible' gold are largely outgunned by a combination of powerful interests and the complexity of its global production flows. While recognising that the task is getting more difficult as the industry evolves and power shifts, we try to illuminate a sensible path forward. In the chapter, we build an argument for placing artisanal small-scale gold mining (ASGM) reform at the centre of these efforts as a tangible and achievable route to making gold work better for millions of people who rely on it for their livelihoods. We also suggest ways in which large-scale mining could be better regulated, focusing on access to both land and capital. When faced with regulating a resource that continues to stoke passions across time and space, a more nuanced analysis of these dynamics becomes all the more valuable.

CHAPTER 2

Gold and the Distortions of Development

For thousands of years, gold mining and the pursuit of gold have been major drivers of development and territorial expansion in civilisations around the world. The quest to extract and accumulate the metal has had dramatic impacts on all fronts – socially, politically, economically, culturally and environmentally. From pre-colonial times, to the 'rushes' that took place during the colonial period, to the 'second scramble' for gold that has ensued during contemporary times, gold has been valued as a commodity, a symbol of power, a currency and a safe haven asset for investment. It has spawned major migrations, having transformative effects on populations and landscapes. In doing so, the quest for gold has both connected and divided regions, in the process stimulating new flows of capital, labour and technology. In his book *The Power of Gold: The History of an Obsession*, Peter Bernstein succinctly summarises the historical impact that gold has had on economy and society:

> Gold has motivated entire societies, torn economies to shreds, determined the fate of kings and emperors, inspired the most beautiful works of art, provoked horrible acts by one people against another, and driven men to endure intense hardship in the hope of finding instant wealth and annihilating uncertainty.[1]

In this chapter, we explore the far-reaching impacts of gold in an attempt to deepen understanding of the profound and complex processes of political, economic, social and environmental change that it has fostered. As a modern-day rush for the resource continues apace, central banks and the ultra-rich are buying gold in record volumes, driving global prices to new heights. This rising demand is resulting in increasingly significant impacts on the people and places where gold is found.

Large-scale, capital-intensive gold mining projects have long captured the imaginations of policymakers and development professionals. For many, large-scale mines epitomise modernisation and development, with the potential to drive economic growth. The United Nations Development Programme (UNDP), for example, has made the somewhat debatable assertion that gold extraction is a desirable driver of economic growth. In 2016, the UNDP argued that foreign-financed, large-scale gold extraction stimulates economic growth and alleviates poverty in poor regions of the world, in the process contributing to the Sustainable Development Goals (SDGs).[2] This puts the UNDP on the same page as the big mining companies. One has to admire the organisation for its optimism. The reality is that the discovery of gold can also bring much misery and harm to the locality where it is found. The brutal and genocidal history of European colonial expansion in Central and South America stands as testament to this.

As such, a number of key 'impact' questions come to the fore. For example, what is the net impact of large-scale mining projects on poor developing countries? What is the immediate and long-term impact on communities that host them, willingly or otherwise? What are the environmental and ecological impacts of gold mining on local populations? And what bearing does all of this have on wider development trajectories and the policies that guide them? In this chapter, we will ask who really benefits from gold extraction and if the resource can be used to drive sustainable, ethical and equitable development.

The next section begins with a brief historical analysis of the early (pre-colonial) impacts of gold, followed by a discussion of its role in fuelling colonial expansion and then its position in shaping global financial markets and contemporary economies. This discussion provides important context, as the historical and ongoing linkages between gold and political and financial centres of power place it in a strategic, almost geopolitical category, which is arguably rivalled in modern times only by oil. This status seems to situate the quest for gold in the realm of 'high politics', with the 'low politics' of social and environmental regulation as relative afterthoughts. And there is ample evidence that this hierarchy of priorities endures today. Against this backdrop, we investigate the impacts of the new 'scramble' for gold, which includes an array of new actors, such as Chinese gold miners working abroad. In doing so, the chapter re-evaluates the evidence for the existence of a 'resource curse', explores issues associated with revenue sharing, outlines the ecological impacts of gold mining, and interrogates the links between gold and conflict.

Gold rushes and nation-building: the rise and fall of empires

By examining the circulation of gold through history, one can trace the flow of power between and within societies. The resource has been a valuable symbol of wealth and progress since time immemorial. While some reports suggest that gold was first mined as early as the third or fourth millennium BC in what is the present-day Republic of Georgia, the first concrete evidence we have of human interaction with gold occurred in ancient Egypt around 3000 BC. In Egypt, gold played an important role in ancient mythology and was coveted by pharaohs and temple priests. Some of the most famous and best-known gold artefacts found in the tomb of Tutankhamun in 1939 illustrate the Egyptians' voracious appetite for gold.

Centuries later, the Romans, who were believed to be the first to develop large-scale mining methods, extracted gold from North-Western Africa and present-day Spain. Gold mining quickly spread to numerous regions across the Roman Empire, and it became the primary medium of exchange and the motivation for further territorial expansion. Gold was both a driver for Roman expansion and a symbol of their dominance.

Long before the European colonisation of Africa, gold was an important resource and medium of exchange in both West Africa and Southern Africa. In Ghana and Mali, in the early eighth century, gold was a resource that these societies traded extensively with countries in North Africa and Europe. The Ghanaians and Malians initially exchanged their gold for salt brought southwards over the Sahara. Later, other goods were also traded within the trans-Saharan network, including slaves, skins, gums, cloth, beads and spices. Gold, however, remained an important material lubricant to keep trade networks flowing.

Colonial expansion: God, glory and gold!

In the fifteenth century, the Spanish and Portuguese initiated European expansion into the Americas and Asia. They justified their exploration and conquest under the pretext of spreading Christianity, but they were also driven by the perceived need to compete with other European nations for territory. God and glory were two of the banners they flew. Another was gold. Colonies were established to serve as resource hinterlands and a pool of cheap labour for European countries, and this source of exploitation became increasingly important in expanding and enriching European empires.

'Get gold', ordered King Ferdinand of Spain, 'humanely if possible, but at all costs get gold.' That simple order, issued by the monarch in 1511, set off one of the longest and most destructive and inhumane colonial conquests in history. The American continent was scarred irrevocably by his conquistadors. Scholars such as Prevost and Vanden have documented how, in the early colonial history of the Americas, 'native gold and silver was quickly expropriated and sent back to Spain in fleets of gold- and silver-laden galleons',[3] predominantly from the mines of Central and South America. It has been estimated that, in 1585, a quarter of Spain's total revenue came from its Latin American colonies and, between 1600 and 1810, 185 tons of gold were reportedly transported from South America back to Spain.[4] By the end of the seventeenth century, Spain's empire in the Americas was arguably the richest and most extensive of the time.

Gold was truly a key driver of colonial capitalism and the development of European states through brutal imperial conquest. To state leaders, gold represented both 'power and plenty'. In the early seventeenth century, the state-building project that most European countries pursued was known as 'mercantilism'. Around the time when the Westphalian system of nation-states was established, war was a constant threat. The common belief among key thinkers and policymakers in Europe was that, if they were to survive, states must industrialise and, in doing so, accumulate wealth and power. In other words, wealth was a means to maximise power, and vice versa.[5] As such, politics directed economic activity. Or at least that was the rationale offered publicly.

The idea behind mercantilism was to accumulate wealth at a time when international trade was growing. One of the core components of the doctrine was the importance of accumulating 'specie' – or precious metals, such as gold. The key to accumulating wealth was maintaining a positive balance of trade. If one bought more than one sold or, more precisely, imported more than one exported, the result would be a net flow of resources out of the country – and into a potential rival's coffers. But with all leaders thinking along similar lines, it would be hard to get ahead. One way was to industrialise, focusing on higher value-added goods, such as manufactured products, that one could export while importing lower value-added goods, such as agricultural products. As Thomas Mun, a former director of the East India Company, famously concluded: 'The ordinary means therefore to increase our wealth and treasure is by Forraign Trade, wherein wee must ever observe this rule, to sell more to strangers yearly than wee consume of theirs in value.'[6]

But another way – a short cut of sorts that complemented an industrial strategy – was simply to acquire specie from home and abroad. The search for these precious metals was not just for riches but could also be seen as essentially a state development strategy. This strategy led to immense misery as lands were occupied in the pursuit of gold, while the people who lived in these lands were more often than not put to work, forcibly removed or killed. It was power politics at its most cynical, with power and plenty marching hand in hand.[7]

During the second wave of colonial expansion, beginning in the nineteenth century, focus shifted to the African continent. In this so-called scramble for Africa, European countries carved up the continent, creating arbitrary borders as they claimed vast tracts of land and great quantities of resources. Gold remained central in this scramble, with an expat-led gold rush taking place on the Gold Coast of West Africa (present-day Ghana) between 1875 and 1900. The discovery of gold in the Witwatersrand in 1886 led to the Second Boer War and ultimately the founding of South Africa.

Around the same time, other gold rushes were taking place in remote regions around the world, causing large migrations of people seeking to make their fortunes. The California Gold Rush (1849), the Victoria Gold Rush in Australia (1851) and the Klondike Gold Rush in north-western Canada (1896–9) all involved the influx of hundreds of thousands of miners, in the process creating permanent settlements in 'new frontiers' while at the same time displacing scores of indigenous peoples. These rushes also played an important role in stimulating new communication technologies and transportation infrastructure, further accelerating the expansion of empires.[8] These developments catalysed new flows of goods, people and credit, as euphoria swept through gold rush landscapes. Meanwhile, at the commanding heights of the economy, gold was consolidating its prominent position as a lynchpin of financial exchange in a rapidly globalising economy.

Gold and power: states and capital markets

Gold has played such a prominent role in the evolution of the global political economy that entire eras of financial regulation are defined by their relationship to it. Take the 'gold standard'. The gold standard is simply a system by which countries peg their currency to gold, making their money convertible into gold and vice versa. So one monetary unit – a dollar, for example – equals a specified weight in gold. This gives investors – anybody holding onto the currency really – confidence they can always cash in their paper money or coins for an equivalent amount of gold. If multiple countries do this, the idea is that this underlying confidence will facilitate trade, as cross-border investors will have assurances that their money can be exchanged for gold at any time. Even better, if other currencies are also pegged, investors can move their money around without worrying too much about one currency devaluing relative to another one.

A further advantage, if you're a trade minister at least, is that the gold standard makes trade balances automatic in the long run – at least in theory. The Scottish economist David Hume argued this in the eighteenth century. He called it the 'price–specie flow' model. The idea here is that, when trade is imbalanced, the transfer of gold from one country to another will help the money supply adjust, which shifts prices and sends trade flows in the opposite direction until a balance is achieved. For example, if a country is importing more than it exports, it will be sending money (and the gold to which it is pegged) to the exporting countries. This reduces the money supply, which will dampen demand for both imports and local goods, the latter of which will reduce local prices and make the country's exports relatively more competitive. The trade deficit disappears and balance is restored. In this way, the international flow of gold should lubricate trade through the capital mobility it nurtures – as long as countries stick to the deal, keeping their currencies pegged and transferring gold when required.

The gold standard worked well for a while, embraced by the world's great powers since the early nineteenth century. However, it eventually collapsed in the interwar years when the world was hit by the Great Depression. There are many explanations for why it collapsed. The economic historian Charles Kindleberger argued it was because Britain was in decline and America was not yet willing to take on the monetary functions Britain once provided, which would have included policing the adherence of others to the gold standard.[9] Instead, the world witnessed a competitive devaluation of currencies and rising tariffs on trade, driving the global economy towards a deep recession. Others, such as Beth Simmons, have argued that domestic politics was really to blame, as governments faced pressure to adjust their external monetary policy instead of placing the required pain of adjustment onto their citizens every time they needed to adjust the money supply.[10] In this explanation, it is democracy and the rising demands of people and unions that led to the gold standard's collapse.

Eventually, at Bretton Woods in 1944, the Americans did accept their role in providing the public good of underwriting and policing the global monetary system. This second shot at the gold standard has also been called a 'dollar standard', as the US dollar was pegged to gold (at \$35 per ounce) and other currencies were then pegged to the dollar. This was a slightly less rigid system and worked well for some time, but eventually this version of the gold standard was also ended, when Richard Nixon halted the convertibility of US dollars to gold in 1971. The main justification for ending this system was the argument that the US would have to run a trade deficit to supply the system, which would eventually become unmanageable.[11] And there were explanations based on domestic politics here too, namely, that Nixon faced pressure to adjust foreign economic policy in a bid to free up domestic policy options and, ultimately, get re-elected.[12]

While gold seemed to take a backseat in global monetary affairs for the remainder of the century, the last two decades have seen investors flocking to the metal, driving the price to record highs. And its popularity appears to have shown no sign of slowing down.[13] This, in turn, has led to the most recent scramble for gold.

The recent scramble for gold

Much more than merely footnotes in history, gold rushes continue to play a central role in shaping contemporary societies, laying the foundations for the economic, industrial and environmental change in the modern world. The ever-increasing global demand for gold has meant that even some of the world's most well-endowed deposits have recently become 'mined out', with decreasing gold content in ores. Even so, global gold production continues to increase apace.

Since the 1970s, the price of gold has climbed steadily. Just over forty years after the price of gold was pegged at US$35 per ounce, by August 2011 its price had risen to nearly US$2,000 per ounce. While many factors have influenced the increasing price of gold, one of the most convincing explanations for its meteoric surge in value is the dramatic emergence of Asia, Latin America and the Middle East into the global economy. As new consumers have gained purchasing power, demand and prices have risen. But emerging market central banks have also accumulated gold reserves to bolster their economies. Over the last decade, the astounding escalation in the value of gold has been an important factor in stimulating the most recent scramble for gold, driven in large part by large-scale mining companies, particularly across Africa and the developing world.

Even with the price of gold soaring, it is far from clear whether or not gold endowments are a blessing or a curse for countries, particularly those located in the Global South, where there is a desperate need for capital and foreign direct investment (FDI) to drive development. More critical analysts such as James Ferguson point to what he has described as 'enclave' extraction, where mobile, footloose global capital is deposited in resource-extraction enclaves. The extraction thus takes place without generating sustained prosperity for a wider region. In such situations, where there are few forwards or backwards economic linkages in the local economy, there are limited opportunities for wider social or economic development beyond the mine. The development takes place only in a localised enclave.

But these rising prices have also directly contributed to a flourishing artisanal and small-scale gold mining (ASGM) sector, providing a livelihood for millions of poor people around the world. As a key component of the recent scramble for gold, the potential of ASGM as a more locally grounded catalyst of development should not be overlooked. ASGM – low-tech, informal, labour-intensive gold processing and extraction – provides a direct livelihood to an estimated 10 to 15 million miners, including some 4.5 million women and 1 million children.[14] Many millions more benefit indirectly from this sector from the forwards and backwards economic linkages that are created. Because of the informal nature of most ASGM activities, accurate data are difficult to obtain. But some estimates suggest that as many as 100 million people – directly and indirectly – depend on them for their livelihoods, mostly concentrated in lower income economies in Africa, Asia and South America.[15] This work also suggests that ASGM is now responsible for around 20 per cent (600 to 650 tonnes per annum) of the world's primary mined gold production. More analysis is clearly needed to explore both the challenges and benefits of the ASGM sector, as well as its potential as a viable development strategy. This is an important topic for future work, and so we address this in further detail in the concluding chapter.

Driven by soaring gold prices and heightened resource demands from the world's emerging economies, the globalisation of the extractive industries has also led to dramatic technological, organisational and regulatory changes in gold-rich countries. Indeed, many governments have adopted new mining codes, or revised existing ones, to stimulate a flood of FDI in gold extraction.[16] In West Africa, countries such as

Burkina Faso, Guinea and Côte d'Ivoire have increased gold production dramatically, and Mali, which had no commercial gold industry in 1990, has grown to become Africa's third largest gold producer,[17] with 71 per cent of export earnings coming from mining in 2012.

In many developing countries, the neo-liberal 'roll back' of the state and privatisation of social services has brought about intensified pressure on industrial mining companies to become 'development providers'. Gavin Bridge points out that large-scale gold mining is no longer regarded merely as a commercial activity but rather as 'a means for territorial modernization'.[18] Large-scale mining projects are often legitimised and justified by host governments with reference to theories of 'big push' modernisation or regional 'growth poles'.

According to this position, extractive-sector investments will stimulate infrastructure development, as well as 'multiplier effects' that will drive economic growth and provide opportunities for resource-rich regions to 'plug into' the global economy.[19] Other commentators have pointed out that the growth pole approach can potentially provide host governments with an opportunity to address some of the expectations of those living in catchment communities, through the use of extractive revenues to promote diversified development projects that enhance sustainable local economic growth.[20] Whether growth poles exacerbate or ameliorate the enclave tendencies of gold mining projects remains a matter of debate.

On the one hand, some believe there is considerable scope for gold endowments to generate significant revenue flows, which could translate into improvements in the quality of life in some of the world's poorest regions. On the other hand, however, it is also apparent that a surge of investment in gold mining has the potential to generate significant social conflict around the adverse effects of extractive industry projects.

In short, the 'second scramble' for gold has galvanised a new interest in the 'resource curse' thesis for policymakers, international donors and researchers. The detrimental impacts associated with gold mining have catalysed localised struggles over the unequal patterns of extractive-led development. Despite the fanfare around gold as a driver of economic development, extractive industry investments have had limited economic impacts in many gold-rich countries. There has been very little 'trickle down' to local populations. As James Ferguson has warned, resource extraction that is concentrated in 'exclusionary spatial enclaves' tends to benefit elite groups, has little impact on wider society, and reproduces the inequalities that often trigger conflict.[21]

Of particular relevance to this polarised debate has been the rise of Chinese mining companies as 'development providers' in poor countries of the Global South. China's growing stake in the resource sectors of developing countries has in some cases been likened to a form of neo-colonialism, while others have applauded Chinese mining investments for spurring on economic growth. The reality is almost certainly a mixed bag. For example, a recent report by the German Institute of Global and Area Studies, which explores the social impacts of Chinese mining operations in Africa, unsurprisingly finds both positive and negative impacts.[22] Likewise, Kevin Gallagher and his colleagues have examined the social, economic and environmental impacts of the latest wave of Chinese mining activities in Latin America and Africa in considerable detail, similarly finding that such investments can have both beneficial and detrimental consequences for host countries.[23] In the next section of the chapter, we turn our attention to the rise in Chinese gold mining investment, which speaks to some of the broader concerns surrounding mining-led development.

Feeding the dragon:
Chinese engagement in the gold mining sector

Over the past two decades, China's engagement in the extractive sectors in South America and Africa has increased considerably. Since Beijing launched its 'Going Out' strategy in the early 2000s, and driven by China's insatiable demand for minerals, Chinese companies have made significant investments in resource-endowed countries on both continents. Many of the commodities being extracted have been crucial for the rise of the Chinese economy; China is the world's largest market for iron ore, steel, coal, zinc, lead, tin, copper, cement, aluminium and nickel.[24] It is now also the largest market for gold.

With the spike in gold prices from 2008 onwards, China has become a major player in gold extraction, both at home and abroad. Having overtaken South Africa in 2007, it has become the world's largest gold producer, producing 426.14 tonnes in 2017, equivalent to just over 13 per cent of the global market.[25] The Chinese Ministry of Industry and Information Technology recently stated that the country has plans to boost annual gold output to 500 tonnes per year by 2020.[26]

Within China, most gold mining takes place in the eastern part of the country, where small and medium-sized companies dominate extraction. Building on its position as the largest gold smelter in the world, reports indicate that the Chinese gold mining sector is actively seeking international partnerships and joint ventures, reflecting the role of gold within the country's Belt and Road Initiative.[27] Between 2011 and 2017, Chinese gold mining companies invested almost US$4 billion internationally in gold-rich countries. With this investment, infrastructural development has accompanied Chinese mining projects in numerous developing countries, including Afghanistan, Ecuador, Myanmar, the Democratic Republic of

Congo, Gabon, Liberia and Papua New Guinea. Through the Belt and Road Initiative, the government also aims to develop a network of international trade routes, targeting vast areas of Eurasia, such as the major gold consuming countries of India and Kazakhstan.

But China's recent plans to expand its influence in the gold mining sector have also included developing strategic partnerships with established extractive companies in mature mining economies, such as Australia and Canada. For example, in July 2018, China's Shandong Gold Group announced plans to expand its partnership with Canada's Barrick Gold, one of the largest gold producers in the world, after having already acquired 50 per cent of Barrick's Veladero mine in Argentina.[28] Some observers suggest that stricter environmental factors at home may have become a major factor in influencing China's desire to expand operations abroad. Most gold mines in China are small-scale in nature, employing the use of polluting chemicals such as mercury and cyanide to separate gold from the ore. With more robust environmental policies in place in the country, it has become increasingly difficult to maintain the operations of these mines in a cost-effective way.

Thus, Chinese participation in the artisanal gold mining sector abroad has also flourished in recent years. In the process, Chinese operators have transformed extraction methods through the introduction of new technology and machinery, replacing the traditional methods of pickaxe, shovel and pan. The use of excavators, bulldozers and wash plants have been commonly used by Chinese miners, with much of this equipment being supplied by Chinese traders. Although this has increased levels of production, it has also depleted deposits much more rapidly and had major environmental impacts.

Nowhere has the increasing Chinese presence in ASGM been more apparent than in sub-Saharan Africa. Tens of thousands of artisanal operators from China have established themselves in gold-rich countries across the continent, stoking ongoing debate as to whether Chinese participation in the sector is a positive or negative development. For example, Gordon Crawford and Gabriel Botchwey have explored the large influx of Chinese gold miners in Ghana, suggesting that much of China's involvement in the sector has been negative, becoming a 'free for all' and resulting in irrevocable changes to the traditional nature of the sector.[29] At the same time, other observers have suggested that the Ghanaian government has for many years neglected the artisanal gold mining sector and Chinese miners have in effect filled a void in an informal economy.[30] The reality is that both perspectives hold merit. In many cases, Chinese miners have formed productive partnerships with licensed concession holders and have provided valuable capital and technology. However, at the same time, accounts of corruption, collusion, environmental degradation and conflict have been prevalent.[31] This has prompted some to argue that China's increasing engagement in the gold mining economies of poor developing countries demands a re-evaluation, particularly in light of the traditional 'resource curse' theories that have been used to assess extractive industry investments in the past.[32]

Gold and the resource curse

In the field of international development, few issues have captured the imagination of economists, anthropologists, geographers, political scientists or development practitioners more than the so-called resource curse. For decades, scholars have attempted to understand why so many developing countries have struggled to harness their natural resource wealth to catalyse development or, following the modernisation theorist Walter Rostow,[33] achieve industrial 'take off'. Although not exclusively limited to discussions about gold, the resource curse hypothesis has framed debates that concern natural resource dependence more broadly, particularly with respect to petroleum wealth and the impact of state-run oil enterprises. Could gold-rich developing countries also be plagued by a resource curse? We would argue that, because of its physical nature, high value-to-weight ratio and challenging regulatory environment, gold remains a resource-curse mineral *par excellence*. This is compounded by the fact that some of the richest gold deposits in the world are located in remote territories in countries that are characterised by weak institutions and poor governance.

Debates around the existence of a resource curse have been broadly located within three main sub-literatures: (1) the relationship between resource wealth and economic performance; (2) the links between resources and civil war; and (3) the relationship between resource abundance and the nature of political regimes.

At the heart of most resource curse critiques are the seminal studies of Jeffrey Sachs and Andrew Warner,[34] who were among the first to argue that developing countries with high ratios of natural resource exports to GDP tend to experience low rates of economic growth. Other analysts have added that developing countries that are rich in mineral resources such as gold are often characterised by civil violence and widespread poverty, particularly in rural areas.[35] Still others have observed that such countries – on account of a phenomenon referred to as 'Dutch Disease' – tend to have poorly developed agricultural and manufacturing sectors. Because of their one-dimensional economies, these states are generally highly susceptible to fluctuations in the market values of minerals. Thomas Heller goes as far as to suggest that, in such situations, economic rents generated from the export of minerals, such as gold, 'induce governments to rely on such flows instead of having to impose taxes on corporate and personal incomes, to allow exchange rates to appreciate so as to dampen manufacturing and agricultural exports, to overspend in periods of high resource prices, and to deplete natural resources without replacing the declining capital stock.'[36]

A steady stream of case study material appears to reinforce the negative impacts of an overdependence on resource extraction. Scott Pegg pulls together a wealth of empirical analyses, which collectively illustrate that African economies reliant upon high-value natural resources, such as oil or gold, have achieved minimal economic growth, have shrinking or non-existent agricultural and manufacturing sectors, and have weak linkages to the wider global economy.[37] Michael Ross adds that 'lootable' mineral resources (i.e. resources such as diamonds and gold that have a high value-to-weight ratio and can be easily appropriated and transported by unskilled workers) tend to fuel civil violence and lengthen existing conflicts.[38] But Ross also notes that, in non-conflict situations, lootable resources can potentially produce more widespread benefits for local people and the poor than unlootable commodities. This he attributes to the fact that the extraction of the former can be accomplished with unskilled labour, whereas extraction of the latter involves both a higher degree of skilled labour and capital. In other words, unlootable resources are more likely to generate revenues for skilled labourers, those who have access to the capital required for extraction, and governments – not necessarily those who need it most.

However, others suggest focusing less on the resources and more on the context. For example, Andrew Rosser concludes from his extensive survey of the resource-curse literature that, although many studies provide convincing evidence linking natural-resource abundance to negative development outcomes, little of this research adequately explores the role that social forces play in shaping different outcomes across cases.[39] In other words, he proposes that, instead of asking why resource abundance leads to negative development outcomes, we should be asking questions about the political and social factors that have enabled some resource-rich countries to achieve positive development results, while others have failed to do so. Thus, institutions have taken centre stage and the main focus has been on achieving 'good governance' in gold mining economies. Thereby, host institutions would promote improved transparency and accountability, particularly around the payments that large-scale gold mining companies are making to governments and the revenues that governments are receiving from those companies. But, given the historical tendency for resource revenues to be captured by ruling elites and, therefore, to fuel patronage politics, contests between national and subnational governments over revenue distribution continue to be common. Corruption remains entrenched in many developing countries; central governments are often resistant to devolving gold mining revenues to the local level or to supporting tax schemes that benefit catchment communities, because this redirects resources that could be captured centrally.

Revenue sharing at the local level

The unequal distribution of revenues from gold mining, and the tendency for elites to capture a disproportionate amount of the wealth generated, keeps poor people poor and creates fertile ground for grievances. The reluctance of central governments to decentralise gold revenues to subnational bodies has a long history. This continues to be a source of ongoing tension in many countries. Some of the most serious triggers of conflict emerge between subnational recipients after revenues have been devolved. The case of Ghana and its Minerals Development Fund (MDF) illustrates some of the potential flashpoints associated with local-level benefit sharing in the gold mining economy.

Ghana is the second largest gold producer in Africa (after South Africa) and, based on its policy of returning a small percentage of gold revenues to the grassroots level where mining takes place, is often held up as a model of best practice. Under the MDF, large amounts of mining revenue have been returned to producing communities. There is evidence to suggest that some receiving areas have managed to use the funds effectively, financing local infrastructure projects and service provisioning. But there are also a number of factors that have undermined the country's success in redistributing its gold wealth and pursuing more sustainable pathways to development at the local level.

André Standing and Gavin Hilson note that, in Ghana, 'mining tends to display complex and at times contradictory social and economic outcomes at the local level; it may raise average per capita income, but it can also introduce new forms of inequality and insecurity.'[40] In some cases, the devolution of revenues to local gold-rich communities within Ghana has caused factionalism and distrust. This raises three main concerns: (1) there is a lack of effective use of the funds; (2) distribution is characterised by poor transparency and accountability; and (3) there is ineffective citizen participation in decision-making. Each of these three concerns is often underlined by a high degree of elite capture, patronage and clientelism, which can negatively affect community cohesion and increase the potential to exacerbate tension and conflict.

A further problem is that the MDF lacks an effective legislative mechanism to govern how the funds are managed. Standing and Hilson note that 45 per cent of all gold mining revenues disbursed to the grassroots level in Ghana pass through the hands of traditional authorities (i.e. chiefs). Although there is an unspoken assumption that funds will be used for community development projects, there are no transparency or accountability mechanisms to oversee spending.[41]

This ambiguity can, of course, serve an important 'political bargaining' function, as central government actors are able to secure the support of traditional authorities at the grassroots level. Nevertheless, there is also evidence to suggest that payments to traditional authorities are frequently used to finance expenditures that do not benefit local communities.[42] This further creates bitterness and mistrust between communities, local governments, civil society and the mining companies. Moreover, reports indicate that there are serious concerns about collusion between traditional authorities and mining companies, which can marginalise community interests and damage cohesion, in some cases becoming a focus of conflict and factionalism in communities.[43]

The equitable redistribution of gold wealth to subnational levels is essential for ensuring that the benefits of extraction accrue to mining communities themselves. But this remains a challenging task, given the intensity of contests over resources in many developing countries. A recurrent issue in the recent history of Ghana and other gold-rich countries in the developing world has been the tension between opposing groups seeking to capture the benefits of gold. Traditional authorities, district councils and elites have all sought greater control over gold wealth, while indigenous communities have endeavoured to minimise adverse impacts, assert claims to identity and land, and, where possible, maximise their returns from gold mining.

Ecological impacts

Environmental damage often comes at the top of the list of the negative impacts of gold extraction. By its very nature, gold mining is an environmentally destructive activity, and, as noted by Hilson, '[f]ew industrial activities leave as great an environmental footprint or are as capable of having as much influence on the wellbeing of a society as a large-scale mine ...'[44] Some estimates suggest that 20 tons of mine waste are created in the process of producing a single 18 karat gold wedding ring.[45]

Since rural livelihoods in most developing countries are reliant on the health of natural resources such as forests, soil, rivers, wildlife and fish, a threat to ecosystem services is simultaneously a threat to the subsistence and income of local populations.[46] Indeed, the environmental degradation and ecological damage caused by large-scale industrial gold mining projects can increase the vulnerability of the poor, exacerbate tensions and trigger conflict. But, equally, ASGM – which extends over vast terrains and is not localised in the same way as the large-scale sector – can be as significant a source of environmental degradation.

In many developing countries, the ASGM sector is unregulated, and it is often responsible for generating critical environmental and health impacts. In particular, the contamination of water and soil resources through the uncontrolled use of toxic chemicals such as mercury and cyanide is becoming prevalent across the world. Millions of artisanal miners in developing countries use mercury to extract gold from ore, as it provides a cheap and easy method for recovering gold. When gold particles are mixed together with sand and gravel, mercury is added to form an amalgam, which binds the mercury and gold together. The gold can then be recovered by vaporising the mercury. For many poor miners, mercury amalgamation is not only simple and cost-effective; it is also often the only available means of extracting gold.

ASGM remains the largest global use of mercury and the greatest source of mercury releases. Some research suggests that, for every 1 gram of gold produced in the ASGM sector, about 1 gram of mercury is discharged into the environment.[47] Overall, estimates indicate that the ASGM sector constitutes 37 per cent of global anthropogenic atmospheric mercury emissions to the environment, causing severe neurological and health effects, particularly for unborn children and infants.[48] With continuous exposure to mercury, a range of health problems can develop, among them damage to the central nervous system, respiratory problems, kidney dysfunction, and heart and circulatory disease.[49] For these reasons, national and international initiatives to reduce the use of mercury in ASGM have proliferated, including the UN Minamata Convention on Mercury, which came into force in October 2013 and incorporates provisions to control the supply, trade and use of mercury.

The Minamata Convention addresses a clear and urgent need for international regulations to recognise mercury pollution as a transboundary concern and to confront the environmental and health hazards that mercury poses for millions of people globally. However, implementing it has not been without its challenges. For example, Article 7 of the Convention states that signatory countries must create national action plans (NAPs) to reduce mercury use and pollution in ASGM. Recent scholarship has revealed some of the limitations of this approach, highlighting the technical, social, economic and legal barriers that must be overcome in poor developing countries for it to be effective.[50] Relatedly, Samuel Spiegel and his colleagues argue that, in order for the Minamata Convention and its accompanying NAPs to be effective at the grassroots level, there must be a shift away from top-down mercury policies that are not grounded in prior consultation and ongoing engagement with ASGM communities.[51] Too often, it seems, such policies fail to understand and address the underlying reasons why mercury is being used in the first place.[52]

Although it is sometimes argued that large-scale gold mining projects are easier to regulate and monitor, as previously noted, they can also have significant environmental costs, including water pollution, deforestation, loss of biodiversity, and soil degradation. For example, 'heap leaching' is a common processing technology that can boost production and lower operating costs; gold mining companies around the world are now using it extensively. The process involves soaking large piles of ore with a cyanide solution. Some of these piles can stand over 60 metres high and stretch over several hundred metres. Although these ore heaps are supported by dams lined with plastic and clay, controlling cyanide heap leaching can be a challenge even under optimal circumstances. The dams can leak, overflow or rupture, allowing the cyanide to spill into the surrounding environment.[53] The liners can also wear down or rip from the pressure and movement of the ore, having drastic impacts on the health of both the surrounding ecosystem and human population.

As was noted at the beginning of the chapter, large-scale, capital-intensive gold mining projects continue to be associated with modernisation and progress, to the point where many governments have been criticised as having a 'large-scale bias'.[54] Some governments in developing countries have been criticised for perpetuating a 'race to the bottom' by engaging in competitive deregulation, in effect turning a blind eye to environmental standards in order to attract the investment of large-scale gold mining companies. Nonetheless, there is now growing recognition that the environmental risks associated with extraction must be mitigated if it is to translate into more sustainable development outcomes.

Even the mining companies themselves have increasingly seen the benefit in maintaining higher standards. In situations where companies, elites and politicians reap the benefits of gold extraction, and producing communities are not adequately compensated for bearing its social and environmental costs, the potential grounds for grievance and conflict increases. Consequently, many gold mining companies now take a more proactive stance in making environmental considerations a central part of their business strategy, not least because they cannot afford to have their operations paralysed by grievance-driven conflict. Indeed, the economic costs of lost productivity resulting from delay are significant, and many extractive companies have embraced the opportunity to defuse potential conflict through corporate social responsibility programmes, also seeing it as an occasion to enhance their reputations abroad and strengthen their 'social license to operate'.[55]

While environmental and social impact assessments (ESIAs) are now enshrined in the legislation governing gold mining in many developing countries, they do not always facilitate environmentally sound forms of development. Significant challenges exist in their effective implementation. Such challenges include insufficient company expertise, a lack of institutional government capacity in the scrutiny of ESIAs, the failure to monitor compliance with rigorous management plans, and weak negotiating powers of environmental agencies.[56] These regulatory instruments may also be misused by politicians and elites to sway political decision-making, by systematically overstating the benefits of investment and understating the adverse impacts. Often, impact studies are financed by the investor, which creates potential conflicts of interest. More needs to be done to ensure that ESIAs are more transparent and do not merely become another mechanism for diverting the benefits of gold mining investments to elite actors. The involvement of multilateral donors in financing impact assessments and further scrutiny from civil society actors can increase transparency, legitimacy and the effectiveness of assessments.[57]

The gold–conflict nexus

In recent years, an informative debate has coalesced around the issue of conflict and its link to natural resources. Conflict can be defined as a process that takes place on a continuum, ranging from low-level tension between competing stakeholders to scenarios where there is violence and a total breakdown of order. And the root causes for resource-fuelled conflict are wide ranging. The Gulf Wars were about the supply and control of oil at least as much as they were about freedom (if they were about freedom at all). Civil strife in West African nations such as Sierra Leone and Liberia has been fuelled by the contest over who will benefit from diamond mining. And the struggle over who controls illegal drug production and distribution has perpetuated bloodshed for decades, from Colombia to Mexico. Resources such as oil, diamonds and illicit drugs are now widely recognised as amplifiers of conflict. These resources can both fund and sustain conflict in developing countries.

Yet, increasingly, researchers and activists are drawing attention to other resources that play a major role in motivating conflicts. Gold, along with the '3 Ts' (tin, tungsten and tantalum), has now been labelled a potential 'conflict mineral' by activists, think tanks and the media. These so-called conflict resources are essential in manufacturing a variety of electronic devices purchased globally, including mobile phones, laptops and tablets. As such, they have captured the attention of activists and ethical consumers at the top of the supply chain. This final section of the chapter will outline and explore the links between gold and protracted violent conflict.

A burgeoning body of literature now suggests that an abundance of high-value natural resources, such as gold, is not only detrimental to development in poor countries but can also have a strong relationship with the propensity for protracted armed conflict to occur. The appropriation and mismanagement of high-value natural resources has frequently been cited as a key factor in triggering, escalating or prolonging conflicts in all corners of the developing world. However, scholarship exploring the links between high-value resources and civil violence has also tended to draw different conclusions from compiled datasets on wars and intermittent conflicts. For example, Macartan Humphreys notes that high-value resources tend to shorten civil wars by facilitating military victories rather than negotiated settlements.[58] Conversely, Michael Ross observes that conflict over high-value resources can make war so profitable that one or more combatants can lose any incentive to reach a peace settlement, a view that is also reinforced by the work of Philippe Le Billon.[59]

The literature on conflict resources is well established, with some sources estimating that, over the past sixty years, 40 per cent of civil wars have been associated with natural resources.[60] As noted earlier in the chapter, so-called lootable resources – resources that are easily extracted, have high value-to-weight ratios and are easily concealed and sold – have increasingly been targeted by warring groups as a means of funding conflict activities. As a lootable resource, gold has been linked to dozens of armed conflicts, implicating it in millions of deaths and the collapse of numerous peace processes. To name a few examples, gold has been connected to recent wars in the Democratic Republic of Congo, Sudan, Colombia, Papua New Guinea and Indonesia. However, while statistical evidence suggests that lootable resources such as gold can play an instrumental role in initiating and fuelling civil war, such studies are rarely capable of explaining why.

A number of scholars have explored the causal mechanisms linking resource abundance to war. Debates have largely centred on whether 'greed' or 'grievance' best explains the onset of conflict. The first position emphasises the economic opportunities that warring factions may have for self-enrichment or for enriching their followers through capturing resources (the greed thesis). Originally developed by Paul Collier and his colleague Anke Hoeffler in their work for the World Bank, the greed model has had significant policy influence on approaches to conflict and security.[61] However, their model has also been roundly criticised as being overly reductionist, as well as failing to recognise the dynamics of change in conflict as a structural and relational phenomenon.

The second position stems from the idea that civil wars are caused by anger over inequalities in wealth, often mirroring the political, ideological, ethnic or religious cleavages that divide societies (the grievance position). Where the unequal distribution of resource rents happens to intersect with these deeper social divisions, the risk of violent ethnic rebellion or succession can escalate and spread.[62]

In both cases – whether driven by greed or grievance – evidence suggests that gold is a resource that lends itself exceptionally well to being diverted into illicit channels, thereby increasing its ability to fund and prolong conflict. These links between gold and conflict have been strengthened by the informal nature of most ASGM sectors. This is particularly so, given that mining activities frequently take place in remote areas where governance is poor, regulatory enforcement is virtually non-existent and elite-capture is widespread. Porous and unregulated borders between developing countries have fuelled the emergence of illicit 'shadow state' economies and fortified the local networks that sustain them. Marilyn Silberfein and Al-Hassan Conteh add that these illicit, cross-border resource flows are very difficult to regulate or contain. Because they are often controlled by powerful private interests, they usually continue to function even when sanctions and embargoes are in place.[63]

In West Africa's Mano River Union region, the illicit trans-border trade of high value resources, including diamonds and gold, has been implicated in regional instability in Sierra Leone, Liberia, Guinea and Côte d'Ivoire. Since 11 September 2001, it has also become evident that the illicit trade in lootable resources can provide both an effective vehicle for international money laundering and organised crime and a potential source of funding for terrorist groups. Beyond its 'lootable' characteristics, gold is an appealing source of revenue for illicit networks for a variety of reasons. Most notably, criminal groups are drawn to the anonymity and access guaranteed by the poor governance of the ASGM sector, as well as the weak institutions and political instability in many of the countries where gold is extracted. But it is the nature and size of the international gold market that is particularly attractive to criminal traders. Because transactions are highly reliant on cash as a mechanism of exchange, much gold trading takes place off the record; 'cash for gold' outlets, where no questions are asked, are prevalent around the world.[64]

The West African country of Mali is an example of an environment where both the formal and the informal gold sectors offer significant opportunities for criminal exploitation and links to conflict. Much of the ASGM activities and trading in Mali are informal, but, after changing hands between middlemen a number of times, artisanally mined gold eventually finds its way into the hands of foreign traders who are in a position to legitimise and 'formalise' it. At the point at which gold leaves the country, the unrefined product is melted into crude gold bars at local smelting workshops.[65] According to research by Partnership Africa Canada, each actor in the chain is pre-financed by supporters further up the chain, and this pre-financing arrangement can also include refiners abroad. Reports also suggest that often the exporter simply carries the gold out of Mali as hand luggage on commercial flights to destinations that may include the United Arab Emirates (UAE), Switzerland or Belgium.[66] For gold that reaches the UAE, it regularly bypasses the country's official due diligence procedures and ends up in Dubai's (unregulated) gold souk.[67]

Malian gold is, therefore, extremely difficult to trace. This is particularly the case as it is frequently mixed with unrefined gold from various regional traders and smelted into primitive gold bullion in the capital city, Bamako, before it leaves the country. The 'functionality' of this system is well summarised by a recent report from the Chr. Michelsen Institute in Norway:

> ASM gold exported from Mali can ... be legally or illegally mined in Mali or abroad, and the delimitations between legal/illegal ASM gold are not easily identifiable once the gold is exported. This means that the Malian informal export system for artisanal gold facilitates illegally mined gold to be mixed with scrap gold, stolen gold or legal gold and to be sold to international buyers, who may or may not divert the gold into the legal value chain. This part of the value chain then easily encompasses a potential for a form of 'laundering' of gold from various origins and legal statuses.[68]

The informal nature of Mali's export system for artisanal gold seems to work well for those who operate in the black market and who do not wish to draw attention to themselves. Mali also attracts substantial amounts of ASGM gold from the neighbouring countries of Guinea, Burkina Faso and Côte d'Ivoire. Mali's porous borders, its weak monitoring regulations, its favourable tax laws and its currency (the CFA franc), which is hard-pegged to the euro, have all contributed to the rise of Bamako as an internationally important export hub for artisanal gold. However, at the same time, this environment poses a major challenge for the government of Mali to harness its gold revenue for development, marking a significant loss of funds that could be used to promote economic growth and the wellbeing of the population.

Associated with the issue of cross-border smuggling of gold between developing countries is the tension placed on intergovernmental relationships as a result of tax avoidance and loss of potential government revenue. The illicit trans-border flow of lootable resources such as gold represents a major obstacle for governments to regulate. Evidence suggests that, when there is even a small difference in export taxes between neighbouring states, smuggling will occur into the country where tax rates are lowest.[69]

In one recent study carried out in Sierra Leone and Liberia by Maconachie and Hilson, the trans-border trade of artisanal gold was monitored at selected borderland sites in both countries over an eleven-month period. The findings revealed that gold was an important mechanism of trans-border exchange, particularly across the Sierra Leone–Guinea border. Many respondents interviewed in Sierra Leone described how gold was used as a form of currency in Guinea. Their close proximity to the border made it possible for miners and middlemen to cross into Guinea and exchange gold, easily and with no questions asked, for merchandise or cash.[70]

Conclusion

In exploring the diverse range of impacts that gold has had on economy and society, both historically and in the contemporary period, this chapter has highlighted the key role it has played in shaping the course of global development. The pursuit of gold has always been a quest for power and wealth. Gold is entangled with centres of power both in the state and in financial markets. One need only be reminded of the power politics at play in the current Amazonian Gold Rush to drive home this point and see the impacts of this entanglement on people and the planet. When we are confronted with the long history of gold as a strategic asset, deeply implicated in both macro-economic decision-making and geopolitical competition, the social and cultural roots of lax regulation start to become clearer. When it comes to accumulating gold, mitigating the social and environmental impacts of the industry seems to sit relatively low in the hierarchy of priorities for those in power.

In reviewing the economic, social, political and environmental impacts of both large-scale and small-scale extraction, it has become clear that many of these challenges are intractable. There is no quick fix to redressing the problems that gold causes. Historically the most powerful actors have been able to enjoy the spoils of gold mining, while the least powerful have endured the full force of its impacts. This story holds true today and, as a result, changes in practice have remained all too rare. In the next chapter, we dig deeper into the question of why exactly the global gold supply chain remains so difficult to regulate. This requires untangling the complex relationships between the structure of gold supply chains from mine to market and the ingrained social relations and industry culture that continue to value secrecy, lack trust and habitually flout any regulatory impulse.

CHAPTER 3

An Intractable Industry

Jake was standing in an old phone booth by a remote service station in the Canadian Arctic when it happened. It was 6 pm and the sun was setting. Jake was forty-nine years old and looked every year of it. His face was deep with creases, grey stubble and tired eyes. He'd been a gold miner in the far north for most of his life, his skin toughened by the cold; still, his fingers felt like ice right now, and, as he rifled through his pocket for a quarter, he had to make some effort to pinch the coin tight between his numbed fingertips. He inserted the coin into the payphone and waited for the call to connect. One ring. Two. The third was interrupted – drowned out – by an engine roar, one all too familiar to Jake. The growl of his own 74 Chevy C10 pickup, which he now saw hurtling towards him. He leaped from the phone booth, throwing himself flat to the frozen gravel as his truck smashed into the booth, crushing steel, shattering glass. Startled ptarmigan exploded from the brush. The ringing was only in Jake's ears now.

We met up with Jake in Vancouver, on Boxing Day 2018, through a mutual acquaintance. It was 11 am, and, while our mutual friend contemplated ordering coffee, Jake sipped whisky. He offered some up, so we joined him. It seemed an appropriate choice when you are being regaled by tales of the Canadian prospecting frontier. When Jake heard we were writing a book on gold, he was keen to hear more about it. But he was at least equally keen to set us straight on what it means to be a Canadian prospector. What the industry was really like. We were eager to find out.

The driver of Jake's truck, when it smashed into the phone booth, was his business partner. He was convinced that Jake was about to cut him out of a deal, which is why he tried to kill him. They had been working a gold mining site in the Northwest Territories, and there was much at stake. Who knows how much of this tall tale is true? But it certainly paints a vivid picture of life on the frontier.

Jake described the life of a Canadian prospector as remote and full of solitude. If you've ever been to the Canadian Arctic, you'll understand. It is empty – at least compared to Europe or South Asia, or most of southern Canada for that matter. When you leave many northern towns, such as Yellowknife for example, and drive an hour in any direction, you will most likely end up an hour from the nearest person. In Jake's stories, there were trucks, dogs, small-scale mining equipment and booze. Always booze.

Jake's stories were entertaining and full of colourful detail. They spoke of a kind of cowboy culture, one that permeates the industry, especially at the exploration and initial development stages of gold extraction. These remote places – in the Canadian Arctic or otherwise – are often far from the reach of the law. Once tales of gold get out, prospectors can descend on mining sites like Wild West cowboys and gunslingers. They bring with them a frontier mentality, and their lives seem, at least in the stories we've heard, somewhat detached from civilised society. If frontier life is not always 'kill or be killed', it is highly competitive.

While communities take root in these frontier spaces, Jake's story also hints at a pervasive secrecy and lack of trust running through them. There is an old joke, sometimes attributed to Mark Twain but varying slightly in delivery and attribution, having been told and retold for over a century. 'A gold mine', the speaker states, 'is nothing but a hole in the ground, owned by a liar.' While obviously a joke, it speaks to an industry that has earned a reputation for its spotted history. And this isn't just the case with individual prospectors or solely at the site of extraction. It seems to reappear all along the supply chain. The complexity and opacity of gold supply chains, combined with the highly unequal social relations driving gold production and consumption, have helped to entrench much of this frontier mentality, or cowboy culture, throughout the industry. Together, these factors make gold extremely difficult to regulate, and in this chapter we elaborate on each of them in turn. We conclude the chapter by illustrating how all of these factors can and did come together in the story of Bre-X Minerals, perhaps the quintessential case study of regulatory failure.

But first we focus the discussion on the complexities of global gold supply chains and how they combine to make regulation technically challenging. These complexities stem from two closely related features of gold: the material characteristics of the substance itself and the structure of its supply chains.

Complexity in the supply and the demand for gold

Perhaps surprisingly, we did not actually know how gold was made until 2017. There were theories, but no proof. In October 2017, an international group of astronomers detected gold being made when two neutron stars collided. Neutron stars are dead stars, and they are extremely dense. One cubic centimetre weighs about a million metric tonnes. When gravity brings two together, they will orbit each other for a while but will then eventually come closer and collide, merging into each other. This neutron star crash creates the heavy elements on the periodic table, such as platinum, uranium and gold. Some of these materials are ejected into space, where they mix with other gases and, eventually, land somewhere, including on Earth.

Of course, matters rather less cosmic bring gold from the earth to the market – most notably, social and economic relations. Picture the supply chain, starting with gold in the ground and then tracing its path through various stages of production until it becomes a 'final' product. Even the final product can be, and often is, melted down and recycled into something else over time, which further adds to gold's complexity, which we will discuss below. But, for now, we can picture the extraction of gold at one end of the chain – the upstream end – and retail items, such as gold jewellery, at the other end – the downstream end. In the middle, we find refiners, who melt the gold into various shapes, sizes and purities, as well as traders who transport and store gold bullion. They occupy the midstream section of the supply chain. Each segment – upstream, midstream and downstream – presents a slightly different set of challenges and opportunities for regulating the industry. It is to these challenges that we now turn.

Upstream
The upstream end of the gold supply chain consists of exploration, mine development and extraction. This is the part of the supply chain that is most closely connected to the localised impacts and distortions of development outlined in chapter 2. Although it would be foolish to attempt to regulate the entire supply chain by concentrating only on this particular segment – ignoring trading, smuggling and the licit and illicit demand for the metal, for example – it is undoubtedly true that this is the point in the supply chain where changes in practices would have the most direct and immediate impact in mitigating the worst outcomes of irresponsible industrial activity. Upstream activities take place within a complex regulatory environment.

Mines are fixed to a territorial location that is dictated by geology, but mining companies are not. Structural changes in the industry that are connected to the policies of governments and capital markets desperate to attract investment have created an industry that is complex and opaque, one in which social and environmental regulations too often remain an afterthought.

It all starts with exploration. A large part of gold mining is, of course, finding out where the gold is, which is where characters like Jake come in. There are individual prospectors all over the world, from the Canadian Arctic to sub-Saharan Africa, Latin America and Asia. Joining these individuals are mining companies that specialise in locating gold deposits. Exploration comes with risk, and, over time, a division of labour has formed between the more risk-accepting 'juniors' and the more risk-averse 'seniors', the latter of which have come to specialise in the more capital-intensive stages of mine development.[1] In recent years there has been a proliferation of junior mining companies, which seek to take advantage of the rather low barriers to entry at this exploration stage and to capitalise on the huge potential payoff, if they get lucky. While price volatility and changes in the regulatory environments have been driving mergers and acquisitions, leading to significant consolidation among the mid-tier and senior miners focused on mine production, junior miners continue to proliferate in the high-risk exploration stage.[2]

Junior mining companies compete with one another over access to land and access to capital. The land falls under the purview of states, while these companies usually raise their capital by issuing shares on financial exchanges around the world. Another route to raising capital is to form relationships with the much bigger and financially liquid 'seniors', which will sometimes supply the capital directly. Eventually, if a potential find is looking lucrative, the junior miners will sell to, or partner with, senior miners who have the capacity to develop the mine site further. But deals and relationships will differ; there is no one-size-fits-all model. While these juniors are important cogs in the industry wheel, they are also the actors most often embroiled in controversy. This is partly because they operate at the stage of production most likely to face community opposition, but also partly because they are most likely to stoke grievances through their actions.

Gavin Bridge has highlighted that juniors are more likely to act unscrupulously since, unlike senior mining companies, they are relatively protected from public scrutiny on account of their small size and lack of name recognition.[3] Tony Bebbington has noted that irresponsible practices also proliferate among juniors, because these companies are focused on the more technical aspects of exploration and consider social and environmental issues as best left to someone else.[4] Moreover, many juniors are poorly capitalised, and there is pressure to discover a deposit quickly in order to recover the investment. Most juniors do not have the resources required to develop a 'social licence to operate' through environmental and community relations programmes. Michael Dougherty's research findings broadly align with this view.[5] He notes that the short-term nature of a mining junior's involvement with a project, before it sells on to a senior company, means that juniors further lack incentive to act responsibly, and this disregard for social and environmental issues is reflected in their corporate governance and culture. Taken together, this research suggests that relatively recent changes in industry structure have led to a culture that is dismissive of environmental and social regulations – especially among firms at the exploration stage.

The entanglement of the industry with financial markets also begins at the exploration stage, adding to the complexity of the gold sector, the lack of incentive for all to act responsibly, and the continuation of the cowboy culture across vast swathes of the industry. Junior mining companies need money to operate, and they raise this capital on stock exchanges around the world. The Toronto Stock Exchange (TSX) and the TSX Venture Exchange (TSXV) are favourites, as Canadian corporate governance and investor incentives favour juniors. Juniors are essentially penny-stocks, and their share prices are prone to wild fluctuations. The potentially high rewards – sometimes increasing in value 1,000 per cent in a very short time – incentivises risk-taking behaviour by investors and the managers of these companies alike. And the exchange itself (e.g. the TSX) has incentives to keep the regulatory and reporting burden low to continue to attract firms and investors. Returning to the research of Dougherty, he finds 'the importance of finance rents leads firms to incorporate in countries that incentivize their junior firms through policy and legislation.'[6] As such, many are legally based in Canada on what at least one financial advisor has called 'the wild west of exchanges'.[7]

Following exploration, the next stage in the supply chain is mine development. Recall that we can actually think of the mining sector as being comprised of two related industries, distinct in the processes they use to extract the gold: large-scale industrial gold mining (LSGM) and artisanal small-scale gold mining (ASGM). LSGM conjures up images that are characteristic of most people's perceptions of gold mining – big open pit mines and monster dump trucks hauling tonnes of rock, as is typical with such giant companies as DeBeers, Rio Tinto and BHP Billiton. This class of mining accounts for most of the market value of gold mining: around 80 per cent. But when it comes to employment, this number is reversed. At least 80 per cent of miners worldwide are occupied in ASGM.

ASGM can take place in either hard rock or alluvial deposits (e.g. those found in the beds and terraces of rivers). It doesn't produce nearly the value that LSGM does, but, as became apparent in chapter 2, it is a vital livelihood activity for millions – perhaps 100 million people worldwide, mining in about eighty countries.[8] Defining what ASGM actually entails remains hotly contested and, therefore, consensus has proven elusive. However, some of the parameters commonly used involve the scale (it is usually small, but can actually become quite large), the permitted depth of extraction (usually less than 10 metres below the surface), the level of mechanisation (low), labour intensity (high), capital investment (low), labour and environmental planning (low) and level of formalisation (also low).[9] In fact, up to 80 per cent of ASGM takes place outside of legal frameworks in various countries.[10] In short, ASGM can best be described as low-tech, informal, labour-intensive gold extraction and processing.

Figure 3.1 illustrates the worldwide distribution of global gold reserves (in the ground). One of the most interesting aspects of this is the fairly even distribution of the precious metal around the globe. For example, each continent is represented in the top six countries (with only Antarctica, where there is a moratorium on mining, missing).

As shown in figure 3.2, it is evident that global gold mining production largely mirrors the countries at the top of the reserves list, with one exception. China leads the pack in terms of gold production and, as we discussed in chapter 2 and will revisit in chapter 5, has ramped up production in recent years, both domestically and abroad. The important point here is that, because gold reserves are fairly evenly distributed around the world, no single or small handful of countries can control the resource in the same way in which other resources, such as oil, have been controlled by states globally. While gold remains scarce and much sought after – giving governments significant leverage over how, by whom, and under what conditions

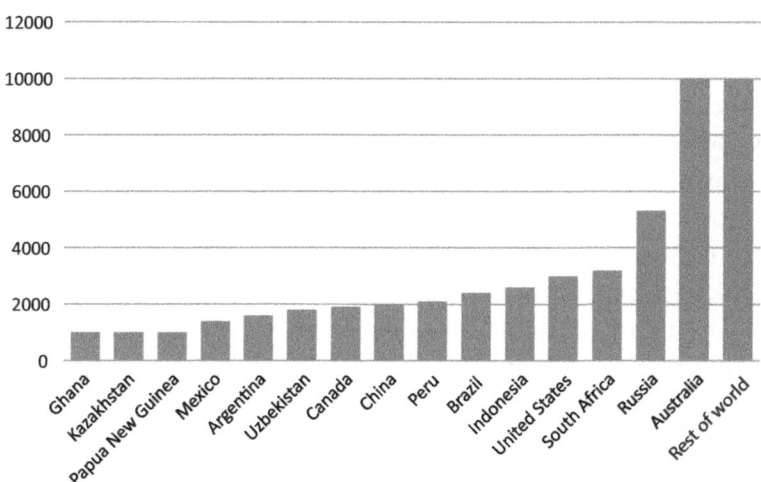

Figure 3.1   Distribution of gold reserves worldwide by country, 2019 (tons)

Source: US Geological Survey, *Mineral Commodity Summaries 2020*, https://pubs.usgs.gov/periodicals/mcs2020/mcs2020.pdf.

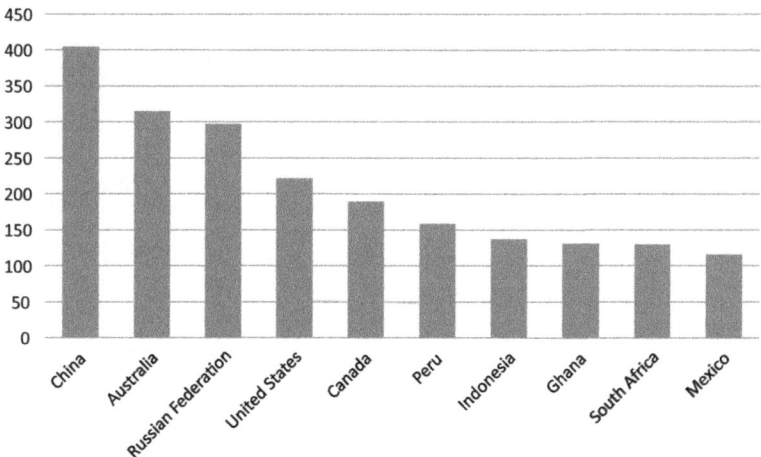

Figure 3.2   Global mine production of top ten countries, 2018 (tonnes)

Source: World Gold Council (2020), www.gold.org/goldhub/data/historical-mine-production.

these resources are extracted – globally mobile capital that is controlled by multinational mining companies also has significant choice in terms of where it is invested. The extent to which mining companies exercise this choice is almost inconsequential. Simply the perception among policymakers that resource-rich countries are in competition for investment gives the industry some leverage over the regulatory environments in which it chooses to operate.

The types of actors working upstream vary considerably. While a single person with a pan or a sluice can undertake mine development artisanally, large deposits are usually developed with the help of engineers, expensive machinery and years of planning. The latter can be incredibly capital-intensive affairs, involving some of the biggest companies in the world (see table 3.1). Some of the names of these mining giants will probably be familiar, even if they do not exactly have the household name recognition of the big banks and retailers that they rival in size.

Table 3.1 Leading mining companies worldwide based on market capitalisation, 2019	
Company, home country	US$ billion
BHP, Australia/UK	120.87
Rio Tinto, Australia/UK	83.98
Newmont Goldcorp, US	32.00
Barrick Gold, Canada	31.75
Franco-Nevada, Canada	17.54
Agnico Eagle Mines, Canada	14.10
Royal Gold, US	8.46
Anglo American, UK	8.33
Kinross Gold, Canada	6.32
Polymetal International, Cyprus	6.05

Source: Statista, Leading mining companies worldwide based on market capitalization in 2019, www.statista.com/statistics/272706/top-10-mining-companies-worldwide-based-on-market-value/; Financial Times, Equities data, 2020, https://markets.ft.com/data/equities/results.

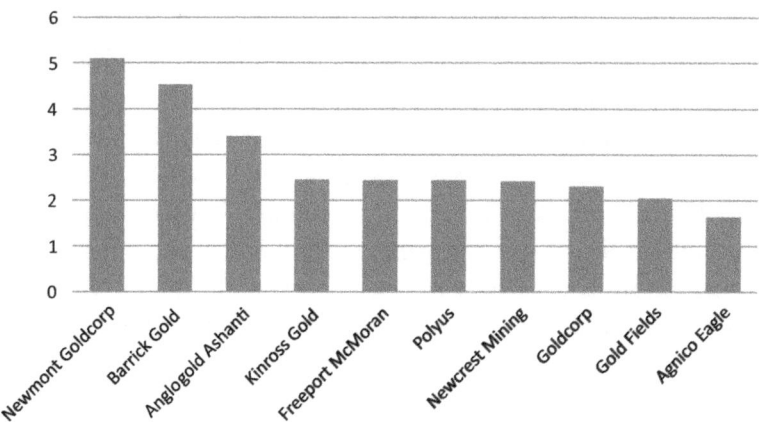

Figure 3.3   Top ten gold mining companies, 2018 (production, million ounces)

Source: Els, F., Top 10 biggest gold mining companies in the world, 4 July 2019, www.mining.com/featured-article/top-10-biggest-gold-mining-companies.

When it comes to the largest *gold* mining companies, however, the names become a bit more obscure, though some will recognise the likes of Newmont, Barrick Gold and Anglo Gold Ashanti in figure 3.3.[11]

The lifecycle of a typical large-scale gold mine occurs in five stages: exploration, development, operation, decommissioning and post-closure reclamation.[12] Combined, the exploration and development stages will take anywhere from one to fifteen years to complete. The mine will then be operational from anywhere between one and thirty years, followed by a phase of decommissioning (one to five years) and mine reclamation (another ten years or so). But all of this, of course, varies with the type of deposit, the processes used, the actors involved, and the specific laws and regulations in the host country.

We have already touched upon the role of mining juniors in the exploration stage and the role of mid-tier and senior mining companies in the development stage of a gold mine. During the operation stage, miners begin the all-important processes of extraction and smelting. Again, by definition, these processes differ between LSGM and ASGM, as well as within each category. These processes were described in some detail in chapter 2. In LSGM, machinery is used to dig up vast quantities of gold-bearing rock, which are transported by enormous trucks to a site for processing. The gold ore is crushed and milled using heavy machinery until it is separated into fine particles. This 'slurry' is then 'heaped' in the pile or added to a vat, where cyanide is used in the 'heap leaching' process. For ASGM, the gold ore is usually dug up and carried to a processing site nearby, where it is crushed and washed to separate the particles for further processing. At this stage, the refined gravels are often subjected to a mercury amalgamation process.

While the gold smelting stage marks the end of the upstream, highly impactful segment of the gold supply chain, it marks the beginning of the increasingly complex stages of production. This is because, when gold leaves the fixed site of extraction, it becomes incredibly difficult to track and trace. Some big mines, such as Rio Tinto's Bingham Canyon Mine in Utah, will have their own dedicated smelter on site, so the ore will not need to be transported far before initial processing. This cuts out some of the complexity in the supply chain, as the mine will have complete control over the ore, which will not be mixed with ore from other sources prior to smelting.

However, smaller mines, including most ASGM operations, do not produce the volumes of ore needed to make such an investment worthwhile; therefore, the ore will be transported to an off-site smelter. Depending on the environment, this means the ore will pass through the hands of a number of traders – with ample opportunity for it to be mixed with that from other sources – before reaching the smelter. Likewise, this can happen with gold doré bars, which are typically about 80 per cent purity when they leave the smelter. Picture, for example, the gold coming and going from the gold market in Bamako, Mali, discussed at length in chapter 2. The ease with which gold can be smuggled (e.g. across porous borders, inside suitcases), the reliance on cash as a mechanism of exchange, the predominance of 'cash for gold' outlets (e.g. in Bamako) and unregulated markets (e.g. in UAE) where no questions are asked, the elaborate financing of smuggling operations from further up the supply chain (e.g. from refiners), and the importance of gold for informal, trans-border trade (e.g. across the Sierra Leone–Guinea border) all conspire to make the chain of custody astonishingly complex and incredibly difficult to regulate. This brings us midstream in the supply chain.

Midstream
The middle of the gold supply chain consists of transport, refining, more transport and storage. This is where it becomes even more complex when it comes to segregating and tracing gold from different sites. It is where practices become less directly impactful in terms of social and ecological issues, but it is probably the most indirectly impactful in terms of stymying regulatory efforts. This is where gold is on the move, changing shape and changing hands. Transparency is low midstream and the incentives to keep it that way are high. It is this muddy middle part of the chain that has been thwarting most recent attempts to govern gold. Whether on- or off-site, ASGM or LSGM, the doré bars are sent via various routes to a refinery, where they are melted and impurities are removed. The gold at this stage is usually mixed with gold from other sources and then transformed into bars of different shapes, sizes and purities to meet customer demand.

In other words, refining is the part of the process where the gold is transformed into those iconic golden bars lining bank vaults in London and Switzerland and government bunkers in places such as Fort Knox, Kentucky. The key to seamless trading in any currency is fungibility – each unit being identical so that they are all essentially interchangeable. It is no different with gold. The most accepted unit of gold is the London Good Delivery bar. These bars are produced by refiners who are accredited by the London Bullion Market Association to produce bars of a consistent quality and to particular specifications. For gold, each bar should be about 400 troy ounces and 995.0 parts per thousand pure gold. Each individual bar is stamped with a serial number, the refiner's 'hallmark' (i.e. a certification of sorts for precious metals), the purity or 'fineness' of the gold, and the year it was made. These are the bars traded on the London bullion market and the ones stacked in central banks and bullion banks around the world.

Because gold refiners occupy the mid-point of the gold supply chain, separating the upstream from the downstream process, they are a crucial link connecting the players at either end. Gold comes to the refiners from all over the world and is then mixed and made into its fungible form as bars. Provenance is rarely, if ever, a concern for refiners, so any remaining hope of tracing distinct units of gold through the supply chain has been all but dashed by the time it reaches the refiners.

Gold refining is a concentrated industry, run by enormous companies. While there are many small-scale refiners around the world, just seven large companies are responsible for refining the majority of all gold.[13] Four of these are headquartered in Switzerland: Valcambi, Metalor, Produits Artistiques Métaux Précieux (PAMP) and Argor-Heraeus. The other three have their headquarters in Germany (Heraeus), Japan (Tanaka) and South Africa (Rand Refinery). Torgny Persson, founder and CEO of BullionStar, a company selling services in precious metals, explains that, although these refiners are headquartered in specific countries, they are truly global entities in their shifting ownership and operations. For example, he notes that Tanaka had just acquired Metalor, which was already owned by private equity companies in France and Belgium, while operating refineries in Singapore, Hong Kong, the US and Switzerland.[14] And this does not even account for the global scope of its sourcing and distribution. Thus, even this relatively concentrated space in the supply chain is complex.

From the refineries, gold is bought by banks, manufacturers, jewellers, gold traders and investors, including governments. But all this gold cannot simply be picked up like items from the shelves of a big box retailer. The transportation and storage of gold is itself big business, and an extremely secretive and high security one at that. Much of it centres on bullion banks, the 'middleman' of the global gold trade.[15] Just like conventional banks, they hold gold for those who have it and offer gold to those who want it. Almost everybody in the gold trade will make use of their services. From vaulting to financing to delivery, they do it all. So a bullion bank will safely keep the gold for large investors such as exchange-traded funds. For large manufacturers of, say, jewellery, the bank not only stores the gold that is needed, it also transfers it to the location where it is required. If a client does not have the cash up front, the gold can be leased for a fee, with the title transferred from the bank once the product is ready for purchase. By leasing gold, protection is provided from fluctuations in the gold price too. None of these services is cheap, and bullion banks charge a premium for their services. They also know how to keep a secret, and one of the big attractions for buyers and sellers of gold is the anonymity that such gold transactions offer.

It is common knowledge that the US keeps a lot of gold at Fort Knox, a military base in Kentucky. The gold is actually held in what is named the United States Bullion Depository, next door to the Fort Knox military base. Fort Knox is tightly protected and synonymous with security. To be 'like Fort Knox' is an idiom for a building so secure that it is almost impossible to enter or leave. Perhaps slightly less common knowledge is that there is a handful of equally secretive and highly secure gold vaults in London as well. The city is, after all, the gold trading capital of the world. But where most of these vaults are actually located remains a well-guarded secret. 'Within the M25' is about as close as you'll get to an answer. The Bank of England is perhaps the only anomaly, with its vaults reportedly located under its headquarters in the City of London. These vaults hold around 400,000 gold bars worth about £100 billion, the second largest holding of gold in the world (the New York Federal Reserve tops the list). It goes without saying that this part of London is under extremely high security; in its 320-year history, these vaults have never been robbed.[16]

There are private vaults in other parts of the city of London as well, with locations more secretive but under equally impressive security. Barclays, for example, opened up a vaulting service to meet the increasing demand for 'allocated' gold. Here, the investors actually buy physical units of gold, whereas 'unallocated' gold remains the property of the bank. Investors seem to be increasingly spooked and want tangible holdings to hedge against market downturns. In 2012 Barclays invited Danny Fortson, a *Sunday Times* reporter, to visit its new facility – on the condition that the newspaper didn't reveal too much.[17] What struck Danny upon entering was the sense of fear such a place evoked and the fortification that was required to maintain security. Electric fences and CCTV cameras are everywhere. In fact, the entire roof is electrified and plinths have been driven into the ground to stop tunnelling. The front door can apparently withstand a rocket attack, while the reinforced steel and concrete walls require pilings sunk 100 feet in the ground to support them. However, perhaps the most ingenious and morbid detail of the security system is that the fingerprint identification system can detect blood supply. It remains virtually impossible to penetrate the premises, even with the use of a severed finger.

From these highly secure facilities, banks can ship gold all over the world. Unsurprisingly, such shipments are also kept very secret. Shipping gold is not unlike shipping large amounts of cash, so security remains high and transparency low.

Downstream

The downstream end of the supply chain consists of manufacturing, retail, recycling and more trading. This is the demand component of the supply chain. Without this demand, there would be no supply. Although efforts at improving transparency have made commendable gains here, the continued complexity of transactions remains a challenge for regulation.

Geographically speaking, China and India consume over half the world's gold, accounting for 30.6 per cent and 27.2 per cent, respectively. The Middle East and Turkey account for 9.3 per cent, while the remaining 33.0 per cent is consumed throughout the rest of the world.[18] Demand for gold is driven by many sectors, though only a few dominate this downstream end of the supply chain. The jewellery industry is the big demand driver. In 2018, for example, it accounted for 50.6 per cent of gold demand worldwide. Investment came in second, with 26.7 per cent of global demand, and government purchasing at 15.0 per cent. Electronics and technology rounded it out at 7.7 per cent of global demand.

If we leave investment and government sales aside for now (we will cover this in further detail later in this chapter and in chapter 5) and focus just on end-use consumer (or retail) demand, then jewellery accounts for 86.8 per cent, while electronics and technology make up 13.2 per cent of total demand. In 2018, the jewellery industry demanded 2,200 tonnes of gold by volume and turned over around US$300 billion in revenue. Indeed the gold jewellery supply chain, like others in the sector, remains convoluted and complex (see figure 3.4).

While gold mining takes place in a fixed territorial location, the creation of a gold ring, for example, is an international affair.[19] Adapting an example from the Responsible Jewellery Council,[20] the gold may be mined by a Canadian company in South Africa, from where the ore is shipped to a refiner in Dubai, after which the gold bullion is sold by a bullion bank to a gold dealer through the Shanghai Gold Exchange, who then ships it to a manufacturer in Thailand, where it is converted to 18-karat, made into a ring in accordance with a standing order, and shipped to a gold retailer in the US.[21] Retail customers shopping for a gold ring therefore have many options. In the US, for example, one can buy a ring from one of around 28,000 specialty jewellers, some of which are independent, while others are big brands. Nonetheless, in this particular market, about half of all jewellery is sold by the top fifty retail chains, so it is rather consolidated.

Most jewellery, however, is sold in Asian markets. In 2016, 2041.6 tonnes of gold was destined for the jewellery sector, with India demanding 514.0 tonnes and China accounting for 629.0 tonnes, compared to only 132.4 tonnes going to the US.[22] In India and China, smaller independent shops have traditionally dominated the retail market, although this too is beginning to change. We will cover these markets in more detail in chapter 5 when we assess the governance implications

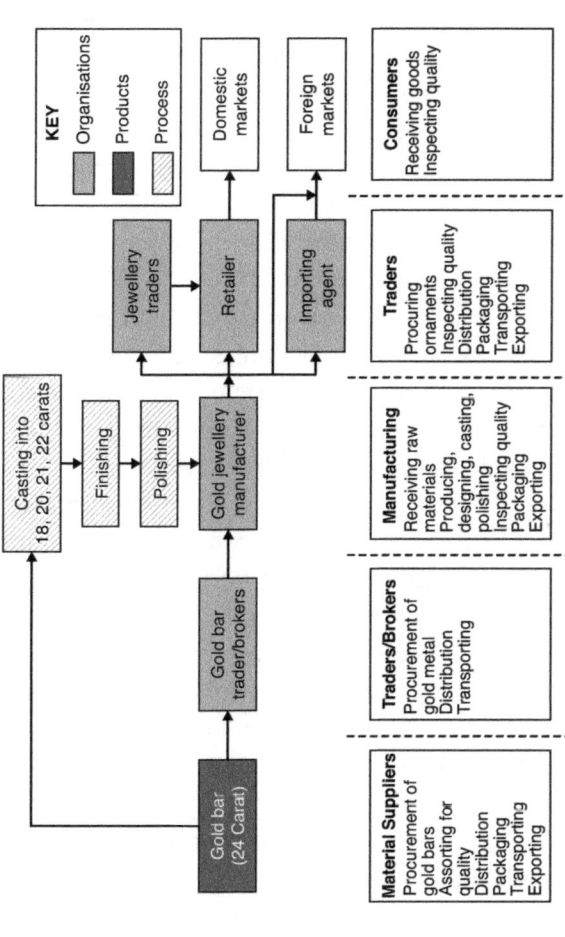

Figure 3.4   Gold jewellery supply chain

Source: Authors, adapted from: Somboonwiwat, T., and Atthirawong, W., Re-engineering of business processes in the integrated supply chain of fine gemstones and jewelry industries in Thailand, 2009, www.researchgate.net/figure/Thailands-gemstone-and-jewelry-Business-Structure_fig1_228433536; Siddiqui, A. H., Sectoral competitiveness and value chain analysis: gems & jewelery, 2016, www.researchgate.net/figure/Figure-5-Gold-Jewelry-Value-Chain-map_fig1_310449618; QAD, Jewelry manufacturing, 2020, www.qad.com/industries/consumer-products-erp/data-sheet/jewelry-manufacturing.

of the recent and accelerating shift in global gold markets. As complex as gold jewellery supply chains appear already, they become even more complicated when we factor in recycling.

'Scrap' gold, or gold recycling, is the final part of the supply chain we need to consider. It injects significant complexity into the supply chain. For all intents and purposes, gold cannot be destroyed. Once it is excavated from the ground and amalgamated, virtually all the gold that has ever been mined throughout history continues to exist in some form on the surface of the Earth. About half of this exists as jewellery.[23] This means it can be melted, mixed with other gold, and formed into something new many times over.

According to the World Gold Council (WGC), an industry group that conducts research and promotes gold on behalf of some of the largest gold mining companies in the world, around 90 per cent of recycled gold comes from jewellery, with most of the remaining amount extracted from electronics components.[24] The flow of scrap is extremely responsive to wider conditions in the gold market and the economy in general. When the economy is unstable or doing poorly, the price of gold tends to be high and there is more gold being recycled. This is not only because people can get a significant amount of money for their gold, for example at pawnbrokers, but also because people are often keen to sell their gold when they need the cash (i.e. when the economy is doing poorly). So recycled gold tends to make up around a third of the gold circulating in the supply chain and has accounted for over 40 per cent of gold in circulation when prices are high.[25]

This further adds to the complexity of the supply chain (see figure 3.5). At almost any stage, and especially in the midstream and downstream segments, gold is coming and going from a variety of sources, being mixed in all the various stages of production, and is therefore extremely difficult to trace. As

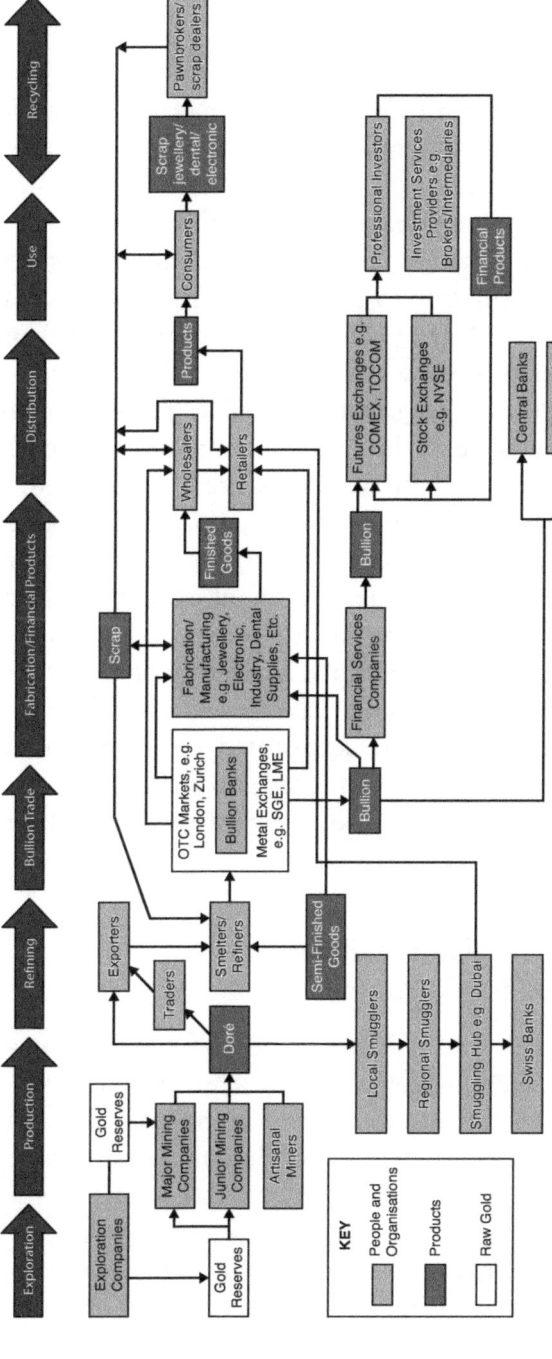

Figure 3.5   The gold supply chain

Source: Reproduced with permission (adapted) from World Gold Council, Gold market structures and flows, 2019, www.gold.org/about-gold/market-structure-and-flows.

such, establishing the provenance of the metal becomes very tricky, and this poses a significant challenge when it comes to regulating the resource.

Its material characteristics and the complexity of the supply chains undoubtedly make gold a difficult commodity to govern. Given this, it is tempting to reduce these problems to being technical in nature. If the problems are technical, it becomes simply a matter of finding the right technical solutions – an exercise in problem solving. But if we reduce problems merely to technical issues, then the power and politics involved in both the problems and the solutions become obscured. We have already seen, for example, the ways in which the culture of the industry itself – especially among the mining juniors – negatively impacts any regulatory impulses in the industry. Likewise, we have been introduced to the incentives faced by financial exchanges to keep the regulatory burden low for miners. To truly understand the ways in which a lack of transparency, lax regulation, and deep-seated social and cultural practices align themselves to make the gold industry incredibly difficult to regulate, we turn next to the scarcely believable tale of Bre-X Minerals.

Gold and regulatory failure: the case of Bre-X Minerals

The way in which gold links to the powerful, its tendency to spread 'gold fever' quickly and leave few immune, and the manner in which the opacity and the culture of the industry all conspire to undercut effective regulation can only really be fully appreciated when seen in action. And what better way to illustrate these difficulties than by recounting the case of Bre-X Minerals. What has been called one of the frauds of the century could just as easily be remembered as one of the regulatory failures of the century, containing all the elements that make gold so difficult to govern.

Bre-X was a mining junior involved in exploration. While somewhat more sophisticated an operation than that of the Canadian prospector Jake, there is ample evidence from the Bre-X case that much of the kind of cowboy culture percolating throughout Jake's tales – and backed up by research[26] – remains firmly embedded in the industry. More specifically, the case illustrates how gold fever spreads rapidly, evidenced by the company going from almost worthless to becoming valued at $6 billion, seemingly overnight, once word of an unprecedented find spread through financial markets. The company then went from $6 billion back to worthless again, almost literally overnight. The find was proven to be a fraud, regulations were shown to be deficient, and the opacity of industry practices was exposed. But not before the links between gold and the powerful, both politically and financially, were on full display. And, unlike the stories we heard from Jake, we know this one is true. It all started in a suburban basement in Calgary, Alberta.

It was 1991, and David Walsh was struggling. He had worked in the mining industry for the better part of a decade, bouncing from company to company before deciding to start out on his own. He had founded Bresea Resources Ltd in 1984, named after his sons, Brett and Sean. In 1989, Walsh launched Bre-X, a small exploration company – a mining 'junior' – as a subsidiary of Bresea. Investors could buy into Bre-X at 30 cents a share, funding the company in its search for untapped Canadian resources, starting in Quebec before joining the early days of the diamond rush in the Northwest Territories.[27] But Walsh didn't have much luck. Penning the company's 1991 annual report in the basement of his family home, Walsh began with the line, 'Yes, we are still in business.'[28]

With mounting credit-card debt and still no big find, Walsh filed for personal bankruptcy in 1993. But he was not done with mining just yet. He decided the problem was that he needed 'a proven gold finder' to help him set up. He had met just such a man a few years previously – John Felderhof. A geologist, Felderhof had been the co-discoverer thirty years earlier of one of the world's largest silver and gold mines, in Papua New Guinea.

By all accounts, Dutch-born Felderhof was a perfect example of those drawn to the cowboy culture of the industry. This swaggering prospector has been described as having a shifty look, a gruff manner and a chortling laugh. Similarly, one reporter described him as a pirate without an eye patch: a hard-drinking, swashbuckling explorer who had prowled the world's jungles, dodging flash floods and poisonous snakes.[29] When Walsh contacted him, Felderhof was snooping about the jungles of Indonesia and, along with his geologist friend Michael De Guzman, was in the market for an investor. From there, it all happened very quickly. Walsh used his last $10,000 to fly out to Indonesia, where Felderhof persuaded him to buy into a property deep in the jungles of Borneo – a spot that became known as the Busang site.

That same year, and overseen by De Guzman, Bre-X started drilling samples at Busang. It was later claimed that many mining companies had tried and later rejected the property as being worthless.[30] De Guzman wasn't having much luck at first either. By December, Walsh was ready to give up and close the property. De Guzman begged for more time. Reluctantly, he was granted a reprieve. Lo and behold, their luck changed. In the following months, the core samples started showing significant quantities of gold. Within a year, it was to reach legendary proportions. In interviews with reporters in the mining world, Felderhof did not mince his words: 'It's so big, it's scary. It's fucking scary!'[31]

By 1995, the company had let the mining world know that they had 'hit gold', uncovering a gold deposit with an estimated 2.7 million ounces of the stuff.[32] But that estimate lasted only a short while. It soon became 30 million ounces of gold, then 60, and later 70 million.[33] Felderhof was not one to dampen the mood: 'Geologically, it's the most brilliant thing I've ever seen in my life.'[34] This is when the so-called gold fever really began to spread.

Bre-X went public on the Toronto Stock Exchange (TSX), and share prices shot up immediately as investors devoured the opportunity. By the summer of 1996 the fever had spread, with stocks that were peaking at almost one thousand times their original flotation price. This put Bre-X's market capitalisation at nearly $6 billion – heady times for Walsh and company. He and Felderhof cashed in just shy of $100 million in stocks around then. The geologist Michael De Guzman went from being almost out of a job to a multimillionaire. They had really hit the big time.

Of course, independent auditors came to verify the find. They noted that some of the gold in the samples appeared a bit unusual. The flecks were more rounded than what one would conventionally find in such a deposit. The shape was more consistent with alluvial gold, the kind usually found in rivers. De Guzman explained that a volcano had essentially 'collapsed back onto itself' 3 million years ago, developing the right conditions for forming the extraordinary gold deposit.[35] Apparently this seemed plausible enough for what was quickly being touted as the largest gold deposit of the century.[36]

A reporter from *Fortune* magazine, Richard Behar, flew out to Jakarta in 1997. Behar marvelled at the elaborate ecosystem that had been created at the site of the find. It was like a Hollywood set with a cast of hundreds, he wrote. They had invested in an airport, provided electricity for the neighbouring village, built a new church, and a kindergarten. They spent over $1 million on social-development programmes for the tribe of Christian Dayaks who formed the majority of their workforce there, even organising sewing classes for women. They promised more to come: a fishery, a poultry farming venture – the sky was the limit. 'You have to understand, this thing is like a 20-foot man,' Chad Williams, a mining analyst, told Behar after returning from the site. He added, 'for someone in our business, it's like taking the biggest Elvis fan to Graceland.'[37] From the local to the global, it seemed everybody had a stake in the project's success now. The gold rush was in full swing.

But, with all this talk of gold, the powerful again sniffed opportunity. Mining mega-deals draw in power and political connections that reach to the very top of the political pecking order, featuring world leaders past and present. In 1996, the Indonesian government abruptly cancelled Bre-X's exploration permit, citing an ownership dispute at the Busang property. Indonesia's President Suharto refused to renew the licence until this dispute was settled.[38] Word was out and everybody wanted their share. And it wasn't just Suharto.

As the gold estimates grew, Indonesian officials were determined, perhaps rightly, to appoint an experienced company as a partner to develop the property. Bre-X was just a 'junior' after all. The mining giants began to compete for the post. For example, Peter Munk, the CEO of one of the biggest gold mining companies in the world, Toronto's Barrick Gold, wanted in on the action. He recruited help to lobby Suharto – none other than former US president George H. W. Bush and former Canadian prime minister Brian Mulroney, who were advisors to the firm. They also had Suharto's daughter Siti Rukmana on board. Bre-X reportedly responded by signing a strategic alliance with Suharto's eldest son, Sigit Hardjojudanto (worth an estimated $40 million).[39] Everybody was hoping for preferential access. And nothing was going to happen without Suharto's approval.

The tale unfolds with the usual cocktail of lobbying, spying, backstabbing and corruption that seems to have accompanied the discovery of gold throughout history. Walsh spoke of break-ins at the Bre-X offices, spies sifting through domestic rubbish, and bugged hotel rooms in which the occupants would crank up the television volume as a precautionary measure.[40] And this was just among the companies. It was corporate competition by any means, and the stakes were high.

But the Indonesian state was also acting to ensure that its interests were served. Originally, the government directed Bre-X to strike a deal with Barrick Gold to develop the property, with Barrick getting a controlling stake of the development company. The government suggested a mere 10 per cent stake for themselves.[41] But they couldn't get it done. The deal fell apart in February 1997. So the president enlisted his friend Mohamad 'Bob' Hasan to help figure it all out. Hasan facilitated a deal between Bre-X and the American mining giant Freeport McMoRan Copper & Gold Inc., of New Orleans. Bre-X was assured the largest ownership stake at 45 per cent. While the story differs between sources, either the Indonesian government was to receive a 40 per cent stake, or Hasan himself was to receive 30 per cent with the Indonesian government getting 10 per cent. Later, when Hasan was asked what he was paying for this stake, he declared simply: 'There is no payment, no nothing. It is a very clean deal.'[42] Either way, that left Freeport McMoRan with a 15 per cent interest in the joint venture.

From here, things began swiftly to unravel. This is where regulatory deficiencies and a general lack of oversight during the feverish excitement immediately following the find became clear. Perhaps as an omen of things to come, a suspicious fire broke out at the Bre-X administrative offices at Busang. Many of the sample and geology records were lost in the blaze. This mysterious fire could have been an accident, of course. But within a couple of months, with fresh contracts in hand, Freeport sent a team out to the Busang site to undertake due diligence on the deposit. This was standard practice and involved drilling 'twin holes' alongside those already drilled to verify the previous samples. They found some striking inconsistencies, reporting only 'minor amounts of gold' in some holes. De Guzman, on his way back to the site to face this new evidence, apparently jumped 600 feet from the helicopter.[43]

The day after De Guzman's death, an Indonesian newspaper reported on the discrepancy between Freeport's independent tests and the Bre-X estimates. Bre-X share prices plummeted over half a billion dollars before making a slight recovery. Investors were clearly getting skittish. The company needed to do something, so they hired mining consultants Strathcona Mineral Services to do a deep dive into the project. In the meantime, the TSX temporarily halted trading of Bre-X. That same day, Walsh spoke to reporters in Calgary, attempting to reassure investors, and told the gathered crowd that he still stood behind their original estimates. When Bre-X began trading on the TSX the next day, investors hammered them. They lost 80 per cent of their market capitalisation in minutes, as investors sensed the severity of the situation.

When the Strathcona Mineral Services results finally did come out, the investors' greatest fears were confirmed. After a thorough investigation, the consultants concluded that the gold 'was falsified on a scale without precedent in mining history'.[44] It turns out the samples had been 'salted'. 'Salting' describes the fraudulent practice of sprinkling gold from other sources into core samples, making it appear as though there was gold there. It seems De Guzman, fearful of losing his job when samples were coming up empty, began filing shavings from his wedding ring and adding them to the samples. But mostly the Bre-X samples were salted with river gold, collected by gold panners between 1994 and 1997. It eventually came to light that, after the initial wedding ring scam escalated, De Guzman began buying gold from the local miners panning the rivers nearby. Over the next three years, he spent about $61,000 on panned gold from locals, salting the samples with 'realistic' amounts of gold – or at least an amount consistent with 'the find of the century'.

If it all seems too easy, it is because it really was. In retrospect, the lack of transparency and oversight was startling. Sample bags are usually sealed off and protected from contamination when awaiting testing. At Busang, all sample testing was done in-house, and the sample bags apparently lay there open for anyone to tamper with. The mysterious fire destroyed many of the records and when, in 1995, some large institutional investors sent in auditors who noticed the rounded edges of the gold, consistent with panned gold, recall that De Guzman fed them a story about 'volcanic pool' theory and sent them off happy. Everybody had a stake in believing the story. None of this was especially sophisticated, nor was it new. The practice of 'salting' brought miners to Canada back in 1567, when Captain Martin Frobisher allegedly presented salted ore to Queen Elizabeth I in order to gain her sponsorship for the expedition to the North. The California Gold Rush saw so much salting occur that purchasers were always on the lookout for the scam.[45] But it seems that, when the rush of gold hits, all previously learned lessons are forgotten.

It is possible that Walsh and Felderhof knew nothing of the salting either. Or perhaps it was wilful ignorance that ruled the day. Nonetheless, De Guzman, Felderhof and Walsh sold off almost $100 million in shares between them, which eventually became the basis of an investigation by the Ontario Securities Commission, which looked into possible insider trading. In the end, despite a number of lawsuits, nobody was ever convicted.[46] In May 1997, the NASDAQ reported that Bre-X had 'voluntarily' delisted its shares from the market rather than have Bre-X officials appear at a NASDAQ hearing.[47] Bre-X was also delisted from the TSX, and then the Alberta and Montreal exchanges, but not before the stock crashed to near-worthless levels once Strathcona's findings were released.[48] The company crumbled into bankruptcy.[49]

The story brings into focus the continued allure of gold. Bre-X's share price had once peaked at $286.50 on the TSX, with a total market capitalisation of more than $6 billion,[50] a growth rate of 100,000 per cent in three years.[51] If the company's gold claims had not been false, it would probably have owned approximately 8 per cent of the world's resource.[52] The Bre-X scandal separated a lot of investors from their money. While its stock had once been the hottest in Canada, the company had left many holding nothing, including the local Dayak people of Busang. Word of 'the gold find of the century' spread far and wide and brought together some strange bedfellows indeed. A dictator's family, ex-leaders of the Western world, and the Ontario Teachers' Pension Fund, through their large investment in the company, were all involved. And the $60 million that Ontario teachers lost, along with money from another 40,000 investors,[53] simply underlines the risk-taking behaviour that seems to consistently accompany gold finds wherever they might be.

Even though nobody was ever convicted in the Bre-X scandal, the entire Canadian mining industry came into disrepute, and its financial system along with it. The regulatory failures that appear so obvious in the aftermath of the saga led to much hand wringing around Canadian white-collar crime and the structure of the Canadian legal system, which was gaining a reputation as a haven for criminal activity.[54] Earlier we discussed the work of Dougherty and others who have argued that both states and financial exchanges will be highly motivated to attract junior miners by creating favourable regulatory environments. Canada and the TSX/TSXV have clearly been very successful in attracting companies, as the two-tiered exchange lists over half the mining companies in the world, which in turn account for about 25 per cent of mining projects and almost 65 per cent of the equity capital raised for mining globally.[55]

In the wake of Bre-X, there was plenty of incentive to tighten up dimensions of this regulatory environment, but not so much that it became less attractive to the mining companies and investors that had made it so successful, namely, companies looking for cash and investors looking for high returns.[56] In the end, new regulations around immediate and independent verification of sites and samples were implemented, making it much more difficult to pull off a scam similar to Bre-X, but also adding extra costs for the companies.[57] Christopher Armstrong, a historian of Canadian financial markets, notes that the financial governance of Canada's resource-driven economy swings between tighter and looser regulation; regulatory failures lead to tightening until accusations of overregulation loosen them again.[58] In other words, regulation is never a one-way street.

The Bre-X story emphasised the continued allure of gold and how this allure, combined with the ways in which the industry mixes with the powerful within the state and markets, can lead to regulatory failure. But the story also holds some lessons for would-be regulators in terms of potential focal points. For example, it demonstrates the importance of access to land and capital for the mining industry. These are the places where one might find some leverage in shaping the behaviour of all the actors involved. The story also reminds us of the continued power of the state in controlling these resources, especially land, and its ability to dictate the terms of any deal, regardless of the global mobility of these companies. The importance of capital markets to companies needing to finance mine development is clearly present throughout, alongside the intangible nature of business transactions that are based on one of the most tangible assets in the world. The fact that the Busang property was, in the end, nothing but a construct at the centre of a massive securities fraud drives home the point that mining is as much about speculation as it is about extraction.

A number of regulatory changes were driven forward in the immediate wake of the experience, but many still contend there is a lack of transparency in an industry that has always valued its secrecy, adding to the already extraordinary complexity of gold supply chains. Although increased transparency continues to be the goal of many industry critics and reformers, we will see in the coming chapters that there is still a long way to go.

Conclusion

In this chapter, we have outlined the ways in which the complexity of global gold supply chains makes it an extraordinarily difficult commodity to regulate. These complexities are related to its physical characteristics (e.g. its ability to be melted and mixed many times over) and the opacity of the industry's processes and transactions (e.g. the veil under which it is bought and sold, moved and stored). But the regulatory challenges are not just technical. Social relations also combine to make gold uniquely difficult to regulate. These social relations are both historical, when it comes to people's relationship with gold, and contemporary, when it comes to the culture of the industry itself. These, too, need to be overcome if we are to mitigate the negative impacts of gold mining. Thus, gold is uniquely difficult to regulate for a number of specific reasons, all of which are present in the story of Bre-X Minerals, an epic case of regulatory failure. In the next chapter, we will focus on the regulatory efforts currently attempting to overcome these challenges.

CHAPTER 4

Gold Governance and Gaps

By now, it should be clear why gold is such a difficult resource to regulate. Challenges in both its governance and its regulation abound for many reasons. It is its physical nature, its historical and cultural significance, its position in a complex global supply chain, its longstanding historical connection to power, and the culture of the industry itself that all make gold incredibly challenging to govern. Neither efforts to monitor and regulate the gold supply chain nor related attempts to establish provenance of the resource and accountability of its users have been straightforward.

In this chapter, we explore some of the most noteworthy regulatory initiatives created to govern gold. While a number of these endeavours have made inroads into addressing key issues present in the gold supply chain, it is apparent that power plays a defining role in explaining how regulations are designed and employed, as well as which initiatives get taken up and which fall by the wayside. Analogous to a gold rush itself, actors from government, civil society and the private sector have raced to fill this space. While some regulatory action has been well intentioned, much has also been an opportunistic colonisation of regulatory space, either for money or for power.

We frame our discussion with the age-old question of where the responsibility of governance should lie – with the state or the market? Against this backdrop, we examine a range of initiatives that span the spectrum of regulatory efforts, from state legislation, to activist efforts, to corporate social responsibility, to certification schemes, to Fairtrade labels, to disclosure regulation in the form of the Dodd–Frank Act. In engaging with the many challenges and innovations in the governance of gold, we conclude that, although there have been some success stories, this has not been enough to truly transform the industry into one in which responsibility is a core concern and an auditable outcome. We begin by outlining the approach of states and international organisations before turning to the various non-state actors and initiatives.

States and international organisations

In host countries, where the gold is mined, policymakers can face pressure from industry, both directly, in the form of lobbying, and indirectly, through the fear of generating policies that scare off investment. In a bid to send the right signals to foreign investors, some governments inadvertently contribute to what David Korten[1] has referred to as a 'race to the bottom', by offering overly generous incentives to mining companies. For host governments, these may include tax holidays, ineffective environmental standards, cheap labour rates, and 'flexible' labour regulation. This can create situations where international mining companies are in effect 'given the keys to the shop' and are able to increase their profits by minimising their costs at the expense of the host country. Likewise, home governments, where mining companies are headquartered, are also confronted with a range of incentives to refrain from regulating their companies operating abroad, mostly around the perceived potential loss of revenues and jobs, reinforced through corporate lobbying. Even if home countries were willing to regulate these companies, issues of sovereignty and jurisdiction come into play. As with other industries and resources, the case of gold shows that those governments in poor developing countries are often most enfeebled in the face of corporate power and market forces.

Whether host governments or home governments, the people making the rules are frequently not directly accountable to those who end up bearing the cost. Many gold mining projects take place on the land of indigenous peoples or otherwise marginalised communities, who are under-represented at the national level.[2] But even when courageous and well-intentioned governments enact laws protecting miners and mining communities, poorer countries regularly face a lack of capacity to keep tabs on the many remote projects taking place in their territory. All these issues are exacerbated when the terrain is dotted with a multitude of small-scale mining sites, which often operate outside of the formal economy. In this highly politicised space, and against the backdrop of a rising demand for gold and the globalisation of the extractive industries, gold-rich countries around the world have adopted new mining codes, or revised existing ones, to stimulate a flood of foreign direct mining investment in their economies.[3]

Since 1985, more than 110 states have adopted new mining laws in an effort to increase foreign direct investment (FDI) in mineral extraction.[4] In most cases, the reform and deregulation of mining codes in developing countries have been implemented alongside broader neo-liberal agendas. But there remains a lack of consensus as to whether or not this has had positive impacts on levels of development. The Canadian academic Bonnie Campbell, for example, recognises that the reform of legal and regulatory frameworks in the mining sectors of many countries in sub-Saharan Africa has led to a much more favourable environment for FDI.[5] But this surge of investment and reform has not always resulted in local-level benefits. In fact, the privatisation of key social service provisioning under neo-liberal reforms has often forced the state to withdraw from its responsibility as a development provider, creating big expectations for mining companies to supply the services and infrastructure that have been neglected.

Such situations have heated up debates on whether state-led or market-led development strategies should be pursued. Many commentators feel that the state should be playing a more forceful role in regulating gold mining investments, in order to ensure that more benefits remain in-country and that communities receive returns in the locations where gold extraction takes place. Some recent evidence suggests that a significant number of resource-rich countries are now pushing back against mineral arrangements that are defined almost entirely by the terms of mining companies; these states could be said to be engaging in 'resource nationalism' in a bid to take back control of their mineral economies. This can include increasing tax pressures on companies, changing contractual terms or insisting on stronger local content requirements. A recent Resource Nationalism Index published by Verisk Maplecroft suggests that as many as thirty countries around the world have seen significant increases in resource nationalism over the last year.[6]

Over the last decade, community development programmes have increasingly become enshrined in the CSR programmes of gold mining companies across the globe.[7] Such arrangements are often regarded as effective mechanisms through which mining companies can obtain their 'social licence to operate',[8] a necessary requirement for doing business in most developing countries today. For many years, such CSR strategies have been voluntary only, and the existence of community development programmes has been dependent on the willingness of the big miners.[9] Yet many resource-rich governments are now changing their strategies, formally adopting laws that force mining companies to pay for, and carry out, socio-economic development projects in communities where resource extraction is taking place.[10] In theory, such community development agreements (CDAs) can provide an effective vehicle for 'locking in' all parties to long-term development commitments, defining mutual obligations and building a shared sense of responsibility.[11] Moreover, CDAs can facilitate the mitigation and resolution of community–company conflicts.[12] This is particularly so in situations where governments effectively fail to provide basic services for resource-endowed communities, and companies are forced to intervene in order to ward off opposition to their operations.[13] However, there is no guarantee that CDAs will actually deliver their intended benefits. Much depends on the context, the design of the CDA itself, and the way in which it is implemented. For example, recent research suggests that CSR approaches which prioritise 'risk mitigation' and corporate public relations often design their community development programmes based on the benefits that accrue to the company rather than on the actual development needs of local communities themselves.[14]

As far as the involvement of international organisations is concerned, the World Bank is at the forefront. Leading the charge for support of the neo-liberal agenda and the dominance of market-led development trajectories, the World Bank has had a long and controversial history of supporting extractive-industry investments in developing countries. For example, Roger Moody outlines how, between 1955 and 1990, dozens of mining-related public-sector grants to developing countries were channelled by the bank through its two sub-organisations, the International Bank for Reconstruction and Development and the International Development Association.[15] These grants were targeted at five main areas:

(1) reform and rehabilitation
(2) 'greenfield' mine construction
(3) mineral processing
(4) technical assistance
(5) engineering work.

Moody reports that, during this period of engagement, the Bank supported nearly fifty mining and mineral processing projects, with loans totalling almost US$2 billion.[16]

Traditionally, the World Bank has tended to prioritise market-led development, encouraging, on the one hand, the private sector to serve as a conduit for development and, on the other, the state to avoid interfering or inhibiting the process. This has often left states impotent in their ability to regulate and monitor mining within their own borders, fortifying the 'enclavity' that is characteristic of so many projects led by foreign mining companies. In 2001, in response to widespread protests from a range of project-affected communities and civil society organisations, the World Bank, under its former president James Wolfensohn, launched its first extractive industries review (EIR) to evaluate the role of the bank in the extractive industries. The review sought to assess whether the World Bank's involvement in the sector was commensurate with its mission of poverty alleviation through sustainable development.

Following the inquiry, a series of recommendations were made to advise the bank on how to make its involvement in the sector more compatible with its mandate of poverty alleviation; these covered a broad range of issues, from good governance and increased transparency, to the adoption of more effective environmental and pro-poor policies, to respecting human rights and the protection of indigenous peoples. In 2004, the bank released its response to the EIR but, while it did agree with some of the recommendations, very few commitments were actually made. Unsurprisingly, the final submission of the EIR was very critical, describing the bank's actions as 'business as usual with marginal change'.

Civil society and the private sector

When states and international organisations fail to govern market actors effectively and mining companies engage in irresponsible behaviour, non-state actors can step into the regulatory space. Among these, the most powerful producers and consumers play a vital role in governing practices along the global gold supply chain, but they are joined by a much wider cast of characters who take on regulatory roles. These are the actors who attempt to change norms, regulate practices, facilitate collective action, and oppose and punish irresponsible behaviour. They operate at all scales, from the local to the global. They impact every stage of production. They come from civil society and the private sector: activists, NGOs, unions, companies and industry groups.[17] We start with the activists.

Because mine production clearly has such potential for social and ecological impacts, there are thousands of activist groups in this space. The majority of these are grassroots community activists focused on a single, unwanted project. Yet there are also 'global' activists who have the resources to advocate on behalf of particular community movements or who advocate for industry-wide changes. Once again, we see that power plays an important role in determining which activist voices are heard.

Global activists – such as Greenpeace, Oxfam, the Rainforest Action Network, Human Rights Watch, the Enough Project and Earthworks – can 'lend' their power to those who lack resources in order to amplify their voices. For local, grassroots activists, linking into these 'transnational activist networks' can strengthen their ability to oppose projects, but it also comes with risks. According to recent research by Matejova, Parker and Dauvergne, governments around the world have begun labelling such groups as 'subversive agents of foreign interests' and used these accusations to justify legal crack-downs and other forms of suppression.[18]

However, not all NGOs are activists in the oppositional sense. Many are advocates of groups within the mining com-munity. There are quite a few groups representing the interests of ASGM miners, for example. The Alliance for Responsible Mining is probably the most prominent group advocating on behalf of small-scale operators and their communities in Latin America, Asia and Africa. They are the group responsible for launching and overseeing 'Fairmined' gold, which is a fair trade certification initiative. For the large-scale mining sector, the Initiative for Responsible Mining Assurance (IRMA), launched in 2017, probably holds the most hope for a true, multi-stakeholder certification of responsibly mined materials, though it is not exclusive to gold. With a membership made up of prominent corporate and civil society organisations, IRMA seeks to certify the mine sites for best practice against a number of agreed upon criteria.

Unions also play an important activist role in advocating on the behalf of workers. Union strength differs across jurisdic-tions, and, in many, the politics can be fierce and bloody. A case in point is the 2012 Marikana massacre in South Africa, where state police shot and killed forty miners during a strike that turned extremely violent. This was a brutal show of state power and the ways in which this power can be been chan-nelled to enforce either the right to mine over the rights of people opposed to mines or the terms on which extraction takes place. In such situations, activists are increasingly opting to act independently.

In cases of perceived government intransigence, one popular activist tactic is to sidestep the government altogether and target companies directly. Instead of pressuring governments to regulate industry, activist organisations pressure industry to regulate itself. These tactics are generally referred to as 'corporate direct targeting' or 'shame campaigns'.[19] The idea is to target companies in the supply chain that are most vulnerable to 'shaming' tactics – such as bad press and consumer boycotts – and use the force generated by these tactics to get them to change their buying practices. The threat to these brands often remains very intangible: in essence, it is simply the risk it represents to the brand, as well as the ways in which such accusations may clash with the corporate culture of the company and its leaders. Yet this intangible threat can and does spur companies to react.[20] In this way, activists can harness the buying power of these companies. When it comes to big, branded firms in consumer product supply chains, this buying power can be formidable. Activists create a market incentive for suppliers to change their practices or, at the very least, engage with the issues that activists bring to them.[21] Within the gold industry, the No Dirty Gold campaign provides a good example of how activists use such tactics, but also the opportunities and challenges such action presents.[22]

Transnational activism: the case of the No Dirty Gold campaign

Earthworks is a small NGO operating out of Washington, DC. The organisation focuses on promoting responsible practices in the mining industry. Concerned with issues ranging from the environmental degradation caused by mine development to the imposition of mines on communities against their will, Earthworks has in the past tackled irresponsible mining taking place on continents around the world. However, despite valiant efforts, it was all too easy for mining companies and governments simply to ignore them. The large companies were too big and powerful and the small ones too hidden from public scrutiny. Governments were often too focused on the revenues from mining to get in the way. In other cases, governments lacked the capacity to regulate effectively. It was difficult for the activists to gain traction.

In negotiating this difficult landscape, Earthworks decided to follow the logic of campaigns in other industries.[23] They would target the branded companies in the gold supply chain and seek leverage through these brands. In the gold industry, this meant targeting the luxury jewellers. Not only had these tactics worked in other sectors, they had seemingly already worked in the jewellery industry. The 'blood diamond' campaign, made famous by the movie of the same name starring Leonardo DiCaprio, also targeted the jewellery industry. The industry had responded, with the Kimberley Process Certification Scheme becoming the flagship outcome.[24] Thus, the activists thought, 'Why not try it with gold?' and began to hatch a plan.

First, the Earthworks activists needed a partner with resources and a reputation – somebody to whom the industry and press would pay attention – so joined forces with Oxfam America. The No Dirty Gold campaign was launched in 2004 and started by targeting the big brands: Tiffany & Co., Cartier, Rolex, Bulgari; it also targeted some of the big retailers, including Walmart, Costco and J. C. Penney. These companies all had brands to protect, especially the luxury jewellers, and the activists were confident they would respond. The activists took out newspaper ads (see figure 4.1), held demonstrations outside

There's nothing romantic about a toxic gold mine.

Leading jewelers agree: it's time to clean up gold mining.

It doesn't make for a pretty story, but the truth is that irresponsible mining practices are tarnishing your gold jewelry. Gold mining is one of the dirtiest industries in the world — it contaminates drinking water, destroys traditional ways of life, and uproots people from their homes. Producing gold for one wedding ring alone generates on average 20 tons of toxic waste. Not very romantic, is it? But there is a brighter side. Leading jewelry retailers are now urging the gold mining industry to make real reforms that respect human rights and the environment. Ask your favorite jeweler what they're doing to support responsible gold mining. If they haven't added their name to the growing list of leading retailers, you can take your business elsewhere. Because when it comes to your gold jewelry, you want nothing but the beauty to shine through. www.NoDirtyGold.org

Retailers who are leading the way:	
• Tiffany & Co.	• Cartier
• Helzberg Diamonds	• Piaget
• Signet Group	• Van Cleef & Arpels
• Fortunoff	• Zale Corp.

Retailers who are lagging behind:	
• Rolex	• Sears/KMart
• Wal-Mart	• Jostens
• Fred Meyer Jewelers	• QVC
• JCPenney	• Whitehall Jewellers Inc.

Figure 4.1   No Dirty Gold ad campaign from *The New York Times*

Source: Reproduced with permission from Earthworks. Learn more about dirty gold at https://earthworks.org/no-dirty-gold/.

stores, and supplied press kits to interested reporters. If they could scare the jewellery retailers into responding, surely they could get the attention of the gold miners. Considering that jewellery accounts for around 80 per cent of the end-use consumer market for gold, it certainly seemed like such a strategy could work (see figure 4.2).

The response from jewellers, and to a lesser extent some of the miners, was significant. Some companies, such as Tiffany & Co., were extremely proactive. The company reached out to the activists before the campaign was even launched and expressed a desire to work together. Other companies, such as Rolex, seemed less interested. But, overall, the industry responded to the campaign and a new governance landscape began to take shape.[25]

Jewellery retailers signed up to the No Dirty Gold campaign's 'Golden Rules' (see box 4.1), a set of principles for better practice. At the last count, 119 jewellery retailers had signed on, committing them to sourcing only from mining companies and

---

Box 4.1 The No Dirty Gold campaign's 'Golden Rules'

- Respect **basic human rights** outlined in international conventions and law.
- Obtain the **free, prior, and informed consent** of affected communities.
- Respect **workers' rights and labor standards**, including safe working conditions.
- Ensure that operations are not located in areas of armed or militarized **conflict**.
- Ensure that projects do not **force** communities off their lands.
- Ensure that projects are not located in protected areas, **fragile ecosystems,** or other areas of high conservation or ecological value.
- Refrain from **dumping mine wastes** into the ocean, rivers, lakes, or streams.
- Ensure that projects do not **contaminate water, soil, or air** with sulfuric acid drainage or other toxic chemicals.
- Cover all costs of **closing down** and cleaning up mine sites.
- **Fully disclose information** about social and environmental effects of projects.
- Allow **independent verification** of the above.

Source: https://earthworks.org/campaigns/no-dirty-gold/retailers/golden_rules/.

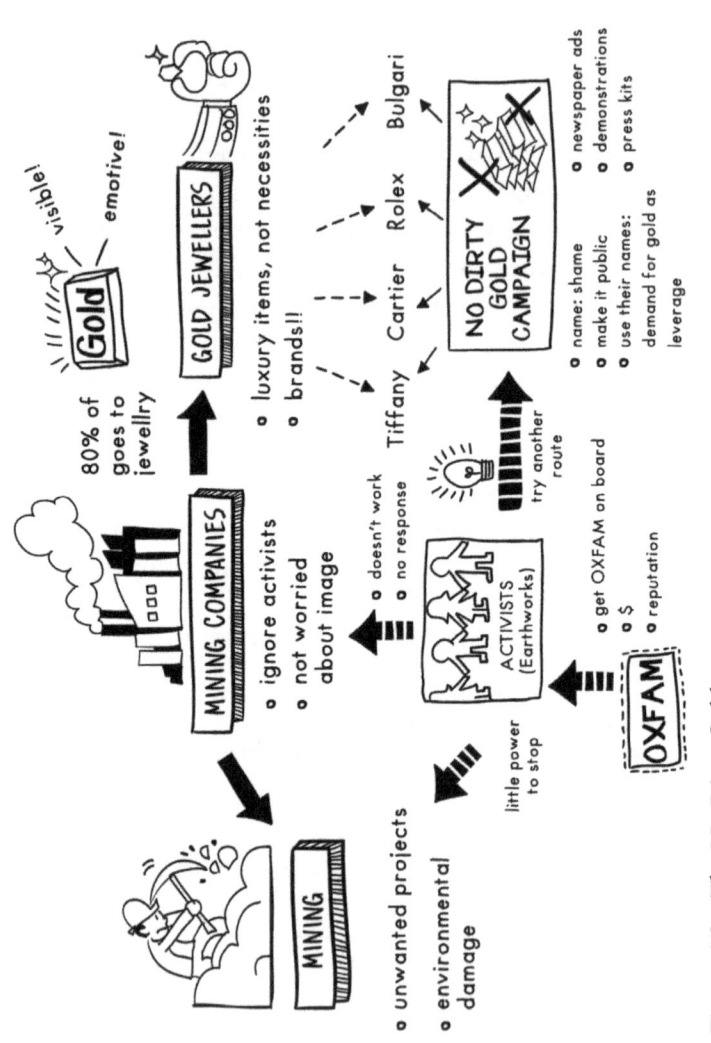

Figure 4.2   The No Dirty Gold strategy
Source: Authors.

operations that followed these rules.[26] While these commitments are non-binding, the principles captured the goals of the activists in a comprehensive fashion and established them as the goals of the industry.

Individual jewellers drafted CSR statements to reflect their concerns and dutifully added them to their websites. But they also engaged in more collective action, forming industry groups to tackle the risk of 'dirty gold' entering their supply chains. The most successful of these has been the Responsible Jewellery Council (RJC).

Created in 2005, the RJC is the brainchild of a collection of key industry actors: jewellers, miners and industry groups. Fourteen of these organisations came together that year and sought a solution to the growing and shared reputational threat that irresponsible mining created and activists amplified. Since then, the RJC has grown in membership, ambition and reputation. But it is an industry-led initiative, and it will always therefore be controversial. Critical observers have accused the RJC of falsely masquerading as a multi-stakeholder initiative, one in which all stakeholders have an equal voice. Pressed on the issue, the RJC's founding CEO readily admits:

> It is purely a multi-sector organisation. A product stewardship group is how we view ourselves. It has much more in common with a trade association than with any other entity. Its membership is made up of companies and individuals who are participants in the gold and diamond jewellery supply chain, and our governance is by those members.[27]

But since its establishment as an industry group, the organisation has taken great strides to increase its legitimacy and expand its scope. It has engaged in consultation with select NGOs, and in 2011 it became a member of the ISEAL Alliance, a certifier of certifications. In 2012, the organisation built on its code of practices and created its own chain of custody system for tracking gold from mine to retail. The RJC has been very successful in its innovation, reputational protection, and growing membership of over 1,000 companies. Clearly, it is doing many things right and effectively responding to a demand for such services. But its board remains industry-led, and the initiative will continue to face scrutiny until this changes.

Opportunities and challenges: a lesson in business power?

The No Dirty Gold campaign has contributed to the landscape of gold governance in many ways. It shows the potential of direct targeting tactics which attempt to hold companies to account, not just for their own practices but also for those of their entire supply chain. A few committed activists have achieved a lot. They have provided information to the industry and to the public about the potentially negative impacts of gold mining. Targeting brands seems to add a certain cachet to the message and gets the attention of both companies and consumers. The activists were also able to introduce norms of responsible mining to the industry when they introduced the 'Golden Rules'. When companies sign up to the principles, they help institutionalise these norms. Slowly, these new expectations become embedded and eventually taken for granted – a far cry from the cowboy culture discussed earlier.

The campaign also led to a rush of institution-building in the form of 'private' governance initiatives such as the RJC and the Initiative for Responsible Mining Assurance. Activists were, in effect, able to create a seat at the table for themselves. In fact, one could say that they built the table. Having been ignored in the past, the activists were now more difficult to ignore. Companies were suddenly willing to sit down and discuss the issues. The activists were slowly but surely identifying allies in the industry, whether they were proactive CEOs, companies specialising in ethical sourcing, or people in those new organisations created to tackle the issues. These allies have been instrumental in helping to create the new, albeit fragmented, governance landscape along the global gold supply chain.[28]

Despite these victories, there are challenges that remain. The actual changes in industry practice at the mining end of the supply chain appear minimal. It is difficult to find evidence that the campaign and its outcome have led to changes on the ground. The campaign drove the issues into the spotlight, but the industry largely took over from there. With industry leading the response, the results have been tempered.

Companies were able to control this response for a number of reasons. We have seen how complex the industry is, and this makes it difficult to trace materials through the supply chain. This, in turn, makes it difficult to attribute blame to individual companies for their sourcing practices. Gold is amalgamated, melted, refined, fabricated, re-melted and re-fabricated. It is traded from buyers to sellers, with abundant intermediaries between. Throughout these transactions and processes, it is mixed with gold from different sources, again and again, through its timeless lifecycle, further complicating the chain of custody.

This complexity not only makes it difficult for activists to attribute blame, it also impacts their leverage over miners in other ways. Even though the jewellery sector accounts for over 80 per cent of the end-use consumer market for gold, this doesn't tell the whole story. We saw in the previous chapter that up to 40 per cent of the gold flowing through the supply chain at any one time is 'scrap' or recycled gold. Even more significant is that over a quarter of all gold is accounted for by investment markets. This rises to almost half of all gold demand if one includes central bank buying, further diluting the market power of the jewellery sector and those who seek to leverage it. The challenges posed by financial markets are significant and will only grow – a dynamic we will explore in much more detail when we look to the future of gold in chapter 5. At present, we turn to two of the most prominent issue areas and the scramble to govern them, assessing the movements to achieve 'fairly traded gold' and eradicate 'conflict gold'.

The market responds:
enter certification and Fairtrade

Because of activist framing and increasing concerns from ethically minded consumers, in recent years a number of certification programmes have been devised to tackle the social and environmental impacts of gold mining, most notably under the umbrella of the Fairtrade Gold movement. Fairtrade is a growing global initiative that aims to promote sustainable development and to alleviate poverty through more equal terms of trade. In doing so, it seeks to change conventional trading systems in ways that benefit poor, marginalised workers in the Global South and to increase their access to markets. The logic is that, through better working conditions and fairer pay, this will lead to social and economic improvements in the lives of the poor, contribute to their empowerment, and ensure environmental sustainability. Fairtrade is probably best known for its agricultural products: bananas, tea, cocoa and coffee. However, more recently, Fairtrade has seen a similar opportunity with gold.

The extent of Fairtrade's involvement in the gold sector is currently limited to ASGM and does not extend to medium- or large-scale industrial mining operations.[29] Fairtrade's vision for the ASGM sector is aligned with core Fairtrade values, including the empowerment of small producers and local communities through improved access to trade and supporting economic, social and environmental transformation.

The Fairtrade Standard for Gold and Associated Precious Metals for Artisanal and Small-Scale Mining seeks to create new opportunities for ASGM operators and their communities. It does so by promoting the formalisation of the sector and by establishing Fairtrade membership-based artisanal and small-scale mining organisations. The aim here is to provide miners with a stronger 'voice' so that they can lobby for improved working conditions, while in the process strengthening their capacities. Box 4.2 summarises some of the key objectives which Fairtrade seeks to help mining organisations lobby for.

Box 4.2 Key objectives for Fairtrade mining organisations

- Legislation and public policies that promote a responsible ASM sector
- Improved environmental management (including mitigating the use of mercury and ecological restoration)
- Social security
- Gender equality
- Child protection and the elimination of child labour in mining communities
- Well-being of families and children
- Fairer market access
- Benefits to local communities in mineral-rich ecosystems
- Improved governance within the ASM sector

Source: Fairtrade Standard for Gold and Associated Precious Metals for Artisanal and Small-Scale Mining, http://fairgold.org/wp-content/uploads/2014/01/Gold-and-Precious_Metals-Standard.pdf.

Fairtrade believes that a fairer and more just gold mining sector will only become a reality if both mining organisations and traders work in partnership and share the responsibilities for ushering in more equitable and sustainable practices. The

Fairtrade standard does not apply to 'gold rush' scenarios or for mining that takes place in environmentally sensitive areas. Rather, it seeks to provide guidance and a long-term vision for the millions of artisanal operators worldwide, serving as a vehicle to support the creation of collective organisations and the facilitation of the formalisation process.

Fairtrade standards are also aligned with a number of other internationally recognised standards, most notably those of the International Labour Organization. ASGM organisations must therefore meet a set of strict ethical labour standards, including maintaining safe working conditions, ensuring that child labour does not take place and upholding women's rights. Once certified, miners gain access to international Fairtrade markets, receive a guaranteed minimum price for their gold, and are paid a premium of US$2,000 per kilogram to fund community development projects. Fairtrade is one of the few organisations that focuses exclusively on artisanal mining, and it has become a global leader in the ethical certification of gold.[30]

Conflict-free gold supply chains and the traceability agenda

In light of growing concerns over the links between gold and conflict in developing countries, a number of recent initiatives have emerged to disincentivise the purchase and consumption of conflict-related resources. Many of these initiatives have focused on gold, given that, once it is melted into a bar (which is easily done at the site of extraction), gold is much more difficult to trace than diamonds or gemstones and there are currently no jewellery industry standards in place to identify its origins.

One such organisation that has been concerned with the traceability agenda – the Enough Project – is a well-known initiative based in Washington, DC, that was originally founded in 2007 to support peace processes in conflict zones in sub-Saharan Africa. In 2016, the organisation shifted its main focus to address the political economy of conflict and combat violent kleptocratic regimes. Also in 2016, the Enough Project launched 'The Sentry', an initiative designed to gather evidence and critically analyse the financing and operation of African conflicts. By engaging with some of the largest and best-known companies in the jewellery sector (e.g. Tiffany & Co. and Signet Jewelers), the Enough Project has lobbied for corporate actors at the top of the value chain to use their power to promote and support the responsible sourcing of gold. Although clearly well intentioned, and having made an impact on a number of fronts, the Enough Project has also been criticised for focusing on a single issue in the mining sector (i.e. the presence of armed groups who benefit from conflict minerals). In its mission to address the problem of conflict minerals, a host of other critical issues have fallen by the wayside, including the widespread problems of unequal labour relations, predatory large-scale corporate investments in the sector, environmental degradation, and state responsibility for regulation.[31]

Another organisation concerned with the traceability of gold – the Responsible Business Alliance (RBA) – has also focused on assisting companies to monitor due diligence compliance. However, unlike the Enough Project, the RBA also engages with actors lower down the value chain, including smelters and refiners, to ensure that their products do not contain conflict gold. Considerable progress has been made, and RBA reports suggest that 101 of the world's 156 known gold refiners have undergone an assessment with either the RBA or other industry groups.[32] At the heart of the problem, according to the RBA, is the fact that there is little regulation at the smelting and refining stage in the gold trade. This is where efforts should be concentrated to ensure that gold is conflict-free. In the words of senior program manager for the RBA, Hillary Amster:

> There are only 330 smelters and refiners worldwide for tin, tantalum and gold ... making it easier to monitor these entities. This is the point in the supply chain where the materials become indistinguishable from other source material, making it the last point in the production process where illicit gold can be accurately identified.[33]

The World Gold Council (WGC) is the most prominent industry group at the upstream (i.e. extraction) end of the supply chain. This is a business association whose main remit is to promote gold mining and investment. Its membership consists of twenty-six of the largest gold mining companies in the world, and it acts in their interest on practically all matters pertaining to the gold market – for example, providing detailed industry information, including market trends all along the gold supply chain. More recently, however, the group has also taken the lead in developing the industry's first 'Conflict-Free Gold Standard' to mitigate the risks associated with gold originating from conflict zones and, importantly for its membership, for companies operating within them.

The standard was initially devised as a voluntary corporate initiative, largely designed to address consumer concerns over conflict-gold value chains. It is aligned with both the OECD Due Diligence Guidance and the US Dodd–Frank Act, and it is also designed to provide support to refiners in meeting their due diligence requirements. The main aspects of the WGC Conflict-Free Gold Standard are summarised below in table 4.1.

Although the WGC's Conflict-Free Gold Standard is, in theory, applicable to all actors involved in gold extraction – including artisanal and small-scale operators – conformance

Table 4.1 The World Gold Council's Conflict-Free Gold Standard	
Aspects	
Main features	Providing assurance gold mined is not contributing to conflict
	Helping mining companies comply with Section 1502 of Dodd–Frank Act
	Aligned with the OECD's Due Diligence Guidance for Responsible Supply Chains for Minerals from Conflict-Affected and High-Risk Areas
Main implementers	World Gold Council members (26) and other companies involved in the extraction of gold
Objective	Providing a mechanism through which gold producers can assess and provide assurance that their gold has been extracted in a manner that does not cause, support or benefit unlawful armed conflict or contribute to serious human rights abuses or breaches of international humanitarian law
Implementation status	Released October 2012; available at: www.gold.org/about-gold/gold-supply/responsible-gold/conflict-free-gold-standard
Sustainability issues covered	Managing risks of working in areas deemed conflict affected or high-risk
	Public disclosure of payments made to governments
	Money laundering

Source: Adapted from: International Telecommunication Union/United Nations University, *Greening ITC Supply Chains – Survey on Conflict Minerals Due Diligence Initiatives*, 2012, www.itu.int/dms_pub/itu-t/opb/tut/T-TUT-ICT-2012-16-PDF-E.pdf.

requires meeting a demanding set of standards. These criteria, as well as the requirement of gaining external assurance, are far beyond the capacity of most artisanal miners. Consequently, the WGC's Conflict-Free Gold Standard has been criticised for having a bias towards large-scale gold mining companies. As activist and ethical jeweller Greg Valerio points out:

> WGC only represents the big mining companies and therefore does not speak for the majority of people working in the gold sector; namely the Artisanal & Small-Scale Miner (ASM). Therefore, any implementation of this process will only benefit

large-scale actors and their subsequent customers. A WGC representative on a recent call estimated that WGC members directly employ around 300,000 across their global operations. This in real terms is less than 15 per cent of people who directly make a living from mining. I know of at least 100,000 small-scale miners on one site in DRC alone, proving the point that ASM is the majority in the mining sector.[34]

On balance, it is certainly the case that the traceability agenda has gained considerable traction over the last decade, reducing the opportunities for armed groups and criminal networks. Traceability has had significant influence on miners, governments and businesses in adjusting their practices. However, many campaigners are still concerned that human rights abuses and the environmental impacts of extraction continue to go unnoticed. In addition, there has been a disproportionate focus on particular cases to the exclusion of others. For example, much research has focused on the impact of conflict gold in the Democratic Republic of Congo (DRC). This has meant that many of the other critical socio-environmental impacts of artisanal gold mining, occurring in dozens of other developing countries around the world, have taken a back seat. But the case of the Dodd–Frank Act and its impact on miners in the DRC also serves as a stark warning of some potential pitfalls associated with the 'conflict gold' agenda.

Disclosure regulation: the case of Dodd-Frank and the DRC

The Democratic Republic of Congo is a desperately poor country that is rich in gold. Some estimates suggest that as much as US$28 billion worth of gold lies under the red earth of its eastern region.[35] The DRC has also been embroiled in a perpetual state of protracted conflict since the dictator Mobutu

Sese Seko was ousted from power in the country (then called Zaire) in 1997. The DRC is perhaps the quintessential example of a state that has fallen victim to the resource curse.

There are now sixty gold mines in the Eastern Congo that are certified as conflict-free,[36] yet, according to the United Nations, conflict gold still provides the greatest source of revenue to armed groups in the country.[37] Estimates suggest that more than US$600 million in gold leave the DRC illicitly each year, with warring factions in Eastern DRC fighting to take control of the mines and trade routes. Some sources also suggest that 98 per cent of artisanally mined gold in the DRC is smuggled out of the country annually, with much of this benefiting armed groups.[38] According to researchers from the Enough Project,[39] conflict gold follows six-steps (figure 4.3) in the supply chain from its source in the Eastern Congo to its end point with consumers at the top of the value chain.

The conflict minerals narrative has been extremely influential in the DRC as an explanation for the profit-driven motives of warring groups and their quest to harness gold to fund conflict. This perspective has put pressure on policymakers, international mining companies and electronics companies to subscribe to initiatives that either ban Congolese minerals from the international market or make their trade more transparent. The best-known of these initiatives are the OECD Due Diligence Guidance for Responsible Supply Chains of Minerals from Conflict-Affected and High-Risk Areas and the US-led Dodd–Frank Wall Street Reform and Consumer Protection Act.

The OECD Due Diligence Guidance constitutes a voluntary code of business ethics, created to promote compliance with international human rights and environmental standards.[40] It provides detailed recommendations to help companies avoid purchasing minerals or metals from conflict-affected areas, most notably tin, tantalum, tungsten and gold. In addition to the

Step 1: Gold Mines: Gold is extracted illegally by illicit miners and soldiers

Step 2: Local Traders and Exporters in the DRC: Gold is transported from the mines and smuggled out of the country

Step 3: Regional Smugglers: Product is purchased by smugglers in Uganda, Burundi, Tanzania and Kenya

Step 4: First Refining Process: Dubai

Step 5: International Refiners: Gold is further refined in Switzerland and India

Step 6a: Banks: Gold is sold to banks as holding gold for investors

Step 6b: Jewellery Stores: Gold is sold to jewellery stores for sale to customers

Figure 4.3   The six steps of the DRC's conflict-gold supply chain

Source: Adapted from Bafilemba, F., and Lezhnev, S., *Congo's Conflict Gold Rush: Bringing Gold into the Legal Trade in the Democratic Republic of the Congo*, April 2015, https://enoughproject.org/files/April%2029%202015%20 Congo%20Conflict%20Gold%20Rush%20reduced.pdf.

thirty-five OECD members, eight non-members – Argentina, Brazil, Colombia, Costa Rica, Lithuania, Morocco, Peru and Romania – adhere to the Council Recommendations. The OECD Guidance represent the most influential and important set of international standards for responsible mineral supply chains, which are referenced, and aligned to, by a wide range of other initiatives, including the Mosi-oa-Tunya Declaration (adopted September 2018), EU Regulation 2017/821 (adopted May 2017), the Chinese Due Diligence Guidelines for Responsible Mineral Supply Chains (adopted December 2015), the Lusaka Declaration (adopted December 2010) and the Dodd–Frank Act (enacted in July 2010).

The Dodd–Frank Act is a comprehensive, 2,300-page piece of legislation that was originally designed to reform the US financial system following the 2008 financial crisis. More specifically, Section 1502 of the Act requires publicly traded companies to disclose to the US Securities and Exchange Commission whether or not they are using certain minerals in their products that originate from the DRC or surrounding Great Lakes Region countries. Dubbed 'Obama's Law' by the Congolese, Section 1502 has, in effect, created a ban on Congolese gold and mineral exports.

While the Dodd–Frank Act has put immediate pressure on companies which mine or buy minerals in the Great Lakes Region to increase transparency in their supply chains, it has also had a number of additional (unintentional) consequences. For example, the stipulation that companies' due diligence efforts must be audited by a third party has resulted in the proliferation of a lucrative consultancy sector, providing conflict minerals-related services in the region. But, perhaps more critically, the ban on mining in the DRC has also had a dramatic impact on the lives of miners and their families at the bottom of the value chain.

The Belgian researcher Sarah Geenen carried out extensive field-based research in the South Kivu region of the country in 2010–11 and observed that the ban on mining had immediately removed the most important non-farm income-generating activity from the rural economy.[41] According to Geenen, this had an immediate knock-on effect on petty traders and transporters, as well as women selling vegetables and school teachers in and around mining areas.[42] These impacts are similarly well summarised by Jeroen Cuvelier and his colleagues, who undertook a detailed study of how the Dodd–Frank Act has affected mining communities in Eastern Congo:

> When referring to the socioeconomic changes attributed to the Dodd–Frank Act, a general consensus exists among respondents. Overall, our interviewees painted a very negative picture of what life had been like during the Kabila embargo, emphasizing the ban's paralyzing effect on the regional economy and holding it responsible for a wide variety of negative developments that have occurred since then, including rising levels of unemployment, school abandonment, armed group recruitment, criminality, insecurity and indebtedness.[43]

In short, the effect of the ban on Congolese artisanal gold miners and their families has been devastating. In an employment-constrained economy, artisanal mining is often the only job available apart from farming or joining a militia group. Some estimates suggest that 1 to 2 million Congolese artisanal miners have been put out of work by the ban.[44] The World Bank uses a multiplier factor of 1 to 6 to calculate the indirect dependents that each miner has, in which case as many as 6 to 12 million people could be adversely impacted by Section 1502 of the Dodd–Frank Act.

More recently, in February 2017, a leaked US presidential memorandum revealed that President Trump had plans to repeal Section 1502 of the Act, on the grounds that its administrative costs were too high and it was having negative impacts for mining communities in the DRC.[45] Although the Republican majority in the House of Representatives has approved a replacement bill for the Dodd–Frank Act – the Financial Choice Act – it has not yet been ratified by the US Senate. Whether or not the new bill will be an improvement over Section 1502 remains to be seen.

Measures undoubtedly need to be taken to improve the quality of life and security situation for millions of Congolese people who rely on artisanal gold mining for a livelihood. Yet some real concerns emerge from the unintended impacts of international initiatives not aligned with realities on the ground. Traceability and accountability schemes that are designed to ensure conflict-free mineral supply chains must have a more nuanced understanding of how the mineral trade in Eastern DRC actually works, as well as the limitations of imposing sanctions in an extremely weak state where vast parts of the country are 'ungovernable'. The relationship between gold mining and violence in the DRC is complex, and interventions run the risk of satisfying ethical consumerism without creating real improvements for the people at the bottom of the supply chain.[46] There are many vested interests in the artisanal gold mining sector, and its informal nature limits the impact of legal approaches and their enforcement.[47] Ultimately, as noted by Laura Seay, 'only political solutions and a strong commitment to security sector reform will produce a lasting peace that enables the Congolese to benefit from their country's rich natural resource.'[48]

Blockchain and 'track and trace' technology

Despite the clear need for political solutions that are sensitive to the particular context at the site of extraction, most global initiatives, in order to work, still need to establish the provenance of gold and track it throughout its journey along the supply chain. It is little wonder then that 'blockchain' technology has garnered so much attention. Across industries, blockchain technology – a type of cryptography that securely records transactions – has been increasingly heralded as a game changer for achieving supply chain transparency. Originally introduced as the technology behind bitcoin, blockchain has been discussed in a variety of industries, ranging from food and textiles to energy and infrastructure, in order to improve supply chain management and traceability.[49] It has also been used to achieve social and ecological sustainability in, for example, the seafood industry, where it has been deployed to tackle issues associated with illegal fishing and 'modern slavery'.[50] Given the multitude of issues associated with the gold production network and the complexity and opacity we have carefully documented, it was only a matter of time before blockchain would be deployed in the mining industry to improve traceability for companies determined to meet the requirements of the various new regulatory initiatives.[51] This interest, including by the London Bullion Market Association, reached new heights when the US refinery NTR Metals was caught accepting billions of dollars' worth of smuggled gold from the Amazon (see chapter 1).[52]

We are still learning about the exact ways in which blockchain might work in practice when it comes to gold, but it is being deployed largely for two purposes: tracing gold through the supply chain and trading gold in financial markets.

In terms of tracing gold from mine to market, the idea sounds fairly simple. Bags of ore can be tagged with a QR code (or an NFC chip or RFID tag) that gets scanned when the bag changes hands. The GPS coordinates where the exchange takes place are then registered in a ledger. As the bag of ore moves along the supply chain, others scan the code, so the product can be traced in terms of people, places and any other information that is seen as important to include. In theory, this allows a person to see the provenance of the gold: where it comes from, who has handled it, and under what conditions it was produced. The main benefit over conventional documentation is that, once the information is entered, these ledgers cannot be altered. They are public (or at least accessible to a particular group of stakeholders when privacy restrictions are in place), so any changes to previous entries are retrievable by anyone who has access to it. This makes fraud and forgery near impossible and should allow buyers to meet the requirements of due diligence reporting for standards related to conflict minerals and similar issues.

The other way blockchain is impacting the gold industry is by facilitating trading. This is essentially gold-backed bitcoin. There are many companies 'putting commodities on the blockchain' in this way. Paxos, a New York-based firm, is one such company. In a similar way to how US currency and the gold standard used to work, Paxos plans to introduce gold tokens that are backed by vaulted gold, giving this cryptocurrency more credibility with its gold backing while also reducing the costs for transactions made with gold and thereby making it even more fungible.[53] The credibility comes with increased security, as the gold and the ledger combine to make it much more difficult to hack than other cryptocurrencies.[54] States and traditional exchanges are also getting into the act. For example, the UK Royal Mint partnered with the Chicago Mercantile Exchange to launch Royal Mint Gold, bitcoin backed by gold reserves at the Royal Mint.[55]

Most relevant to our discussion here are those initiatives attempting to combine the benefits of traceability and fungibility that blockchain offers. Emergent Technology, in collaboration with the mining company Yamana Gold, has been developing 'Responsible Gold', which are digital tokens backed by 'conflict-free gold', ensured through blockchain technology. As a potentially lucrative business opportunity, many more initiatives are emerging at the downstream end of the supply chain, such as 'Trustchain' in the jewellery industry.[56] Blockchain is already widely used in the approximately half a trillion dollar per year semi-conductor industry, so a proliferation of responsible gold sourcing technologies looks likely to materialise here too.[57]

While there is much to be excited about, blockchain is no panacea when it comes to regulating gold. For example, once the gold is on the blockchain, it can be traced. But there remains what has been called a 'first mile' problem, which refers to tracking the gold before it enters the ledger.[58] At this point, the person carrying the gold still needs to be relied upon to declare its provenance accurately. But this is simply a technical issue. The really sticky issues are the political ones. Filipe Calvão and Victoria Gronwald have studied the opportunities and risks of the introduction of this new technology for mining communities in Africa.[59] According to their findings, it is not yet clear what the benefits of this technology will be for ASGM miners and their communities, and it could potentially end up excluding miners through the high costs and inaccessibility of the technology and data. As with many of these regulatory solutions, it is easier to identify the ways in which the choice of response benefits the most powerful actors in the supply chain than to recognise how it might benefit the least powerful.

Conclusion: can 'ethical gold' make a difference?

In this chapter, it has become clear that efforts to monitor and regulate the gold supply chain have not been straightforward.

In exploring some of the best-known regulatory initiatives that have been implemented to govern gold, we have engaged with the numerous challenges that must be confronted. While there have indeed been pockets of success, many initiatives have failed to achieve their intended outcomes and have fallen far short of being transformational.

For example, although the Fairtrade Standard for Gold has made significant inroads into addressing the unequal nature of the artisanal gold value chain, it has not been without its critics. Some commentators have suggested that Fairtrade has 'sold out' on its principles and given in to the market. Other critics have argued that it has distorted markets, exaggerated its benefits, priced out the poorest producers and, in some cases, perpetuated inefficient modes of production.[60] Still others have suggested that the benefits derived through the Fairtrade system are not equally distributed because the certification system is biased against the poorest developing countries on a number of fronts.[61]

First, there are significant cost considerations related to the Fairtrade certification process that can exclude the poorest producers. The costs of certification are, in theory, the same everywhere, yet they are relatively more expensive for those in poorer countries, making the scheme out of reach for some. Second, because of its sliding-scale price structure, certification is less costly for large producer organisations than for smaller ones. And, finally, the cost of compliance with Fairtrade standards is higher for small organisations on account of their lower productivity and smaller economies of scale.

But Fairtrade is far from the only game in town. A number of other ethical initiatives have also been established to meet the global demand for more socially and environmentally responsible mining. We discussed the Responsible Jewellery Council (RJC), for example, which has devised two sets of standards:

the Code of Practices, which must be followed by all members of the RJC; and the Chain of Custody Standard, which is voluntary. We also noted that the RJC has been the subject of a number of criticisms. Above all, critics are most concerned with the fact that the RJC is an industry initiative which does not make its audits publicly available.[62] External stakeholders are able to access only basic data about RJC members, and there is little information available about the findings and corrective actions of the audits. This makes it difficult for external stakeholders to assess an RJC member company effectively.

A number of RJC members have been at the centre of controversy. For example, the international gold mining company Rio Tinto is a member of the RJC, even though its reputation has been plagued by accusations of environmental and human rights abuses.[63] Likewise, the gold refinery Argor-Heraeus SA has RJC membership, despite the fact that it has been under investigation in Switzerland for buying gold from an illegal armed group in the Democratic Republic of Congo. Two other RJC members, MKS Finance and its subsidiary PAMP, both Swiss gold-processing firms, have been accused of buying gold from illegal miners in the Peruvian Amazon, where the rainforest is being decimated.

On the one hand, large certification schemes such as the RJC often have difficulty tracking gold from mine to market. This can allow non-compliant cases to slip through. Thus, membership of the RJC does not necessarily ensure responsible sourcing by a company. RJC's governance, standards and auditing procedures lack the transparency needed to ensure confidence in recommendations. On the other hand, smaller certification schemes, such as Fairtrade gold or Fairmined gold of the Alliance for Responsible Mining, tend to have more success in fulfilling their mandates but will struggle to scale up. Regardless of the size of the initiative, any potential lack of transparency in the auditing process can undermine confidence in certification processes, making it difficult for external stakeholders to assess a company's performance.[64] Innovative disclosure regulation and track and trace technologies are being developed to improve governance performance, but these too have significant downsides that will need to be addressed.

In the next chapter, we turn to the future of gold, focusing on recent global shifts that suggest that the metal is likely to become even more difficult to regulate. This will particularly be the case as markets and centres of power shift to the East. Increasing demand for gold from consumers, companies and governments, and its demand as a preferred financial instrument, will place new stress on governance mechanisms and continue to challenge them like never before.

CHAPTER 5

Rising Powers in Supply and Demand

Given the governance challenges posed by the complexity and opacity of the gold market, it is perhaps no wonder that so many gaps remain in the regulatory infrastructure. The last chapter outlined the multitude of skilled and well-intentioned people and organisations working to address the many issues associated with gold production and consumption. But the most powerful actors in the sector are significantly outgunning these would-be regulators. And it appears this situation is only becoming more difficult. The rapidly changing geopolitical economy of gold seems destined to introduce new issues and ratchet up existing challenges further still.

In this penultimate chapter, we focus on these global shifts in the market for gold and explore their potential for rendering gold even more ungovernable than is currently the case. We begin by showing how financialisation is adding further complexity by introducing new actors and new instruments to financial markets for gold. This, in turn, makes it increasingly difficult to make links between producers and consumers, and between supply chain actors and the impact of their production and consumption decisions. We then highlight the emergence of the BRICS countries as relatively new players in the global gold market. While gold is not new to any of these regions, these countries are angling to increase their role in the global political economy of gold. Zooming in on the two largest markets for gold – China and India – we trace the contours of these expanding markets and their growing involvement in how gold is governed globally. We conclude by assessing the implications of these rapid and large-scale shifts for the future of gold governance.

Financialisation and financial markets for gold

The demand for gold has never been as high as it is today. According to the WGC, global investment demand for gold has grown by an average of 18 per cent each year for the last two decades.[1] Part of the reason for this meteoric growth can be attributed to gold making a comeback as a financial instrument in the wake of the global financial crisis (GFC) of 2007–8. This is because gold helps to manage risk in investment markets, as it is widely considered a counter-cyclical and, therefore, 'safe haven' asset.[2] The popularity of gold has therefore become increasingly apparent with central banks in emerging economies, which have become progressively wealthy in recent years and are storing more and more of their growing reserves in the form of gold. In fact, emerging market central banks have collectively tripled their gold holdings over the past decade.[3]

But rising demand is not simply a result of governments hoarding gold; it has also become a popular asset across different classes of investors. It is worth reflecting on why gold is so popular as a financial asset, on what impacts its price, and what shapes the dynamics of gold trading in financial markets. These factors all influence the supply and demand of gold and hold profound consequences for people and the planet. More specifically, there is a need to consider how global financial transactions – both those involving gold bullion and those nebulous financial derivatives linked to gold in its solid form – are not only helping to drive gold demand but also having additional knock-on effects. Such transactions are adding further complexity to gold supply chains, creating anonymity for those trading in gold and confounding attempts to impose accountability in globalised production.

Investment accounts for roughly half the demand for gold, and probably the number one reason why investors turn to gold is that it helps them hedge against market downturns. Demand for gold tends to rise when markets are unstable or there is potential for a downturn in the near future, but prices tend to be modest when the market is strong. This is all evidence – and a self-fulfilling prophecy of sorts – underscoring that investors see gold as a safer way than currencies to hold their assets. Gold is easy to sell, and discreetly at that, so it should come as no surprise that about US$200 billion worth of gold is traded per day in over-the-counter markets, according to the World Gold Council.[4]

In chapter 3, we explored how the sheer number of transactions, intermediaries and instruments in the gold supply chain make it extremely complicated. With the increasing financialisation of the industry, this regulatory hurdle is only becoming more of a challenge. As Jennifer Clapp has found in her research on food, financialisation adds an extra layer of complexity to global production and, in effect, creates barriers for those attempting to make links between particular people or organisations and the impacts of their consumption decisions.[5] In other words, it becomes harder to find out who is buying irresponsibly sourced gold because it is extremely difficult to determine a) where gold originates from; b) how it was produced; and c) who bought it. The more people, products and transactions there are, the more difficult it becomes to make connections. Through these mechanisms, financial markets can essentially delink production and consumption decisions from the physical commodity itself through the trade in derivatives.[6] This makes it extremely challenging for those attempting to establish the provenance of gold – which matters in terms of linking particular purchases to particular practices – as activists and, increasingly governments, have tried to do (see chapter 4).

The price of gold will also impact the complexity of the gold supply chain, indirectly implicating financial markets. For example, when gold prices shot up in the wake of the GFC of 2007–8, the price of the 'scrap' supply of gold followed suit. Recall that 'scrap' simply refers to gold items – usually jewellery and coins – that are 'recycled' through the system, often via pawnshops and related businesses. Of course, the financial crisis also hit people in the pocket, which further incentivised the sale of gold. Gold 'scrap' accounted for about 42 per cent of the gold supply chain in 2010.[7] With all this additional gold in circulation, being melted, mixed, traded, fabricated and melted again, the supply chain becomes very complex indeed.

There are many ways to invest in gold. Purchasing physical assets (e.g. jewellery, coins, bars) is only growing in popularity, as is buying shares in gold mining companies. In chapter 3, we discussed the high-risk, high-reward juniors market, but there are also safer ways to invest in gold mining companies. As the WGC advises, these mining company stocks may correlate with the price of gold, but they are also linked to expectations about the future earnings of the company. This, in turn, is linked to the wealth of a company's reserves, current and future projects, production costs, and management track record.[8] With over 300 publicly traded gold mining companies, ranging from very small to incredibly large, there are many to choose from. There are also many indices providing information on a company's performance, including the FTSE Gold Mines Index, the S&P/TSX Capped Gold Index, the Philadelphia Gold and Silver Index, and the NYSE Arca Gold BUGS Index.[9]

But many investors increasingly place their confidence in a large and growing basket of gold investment instruments. Investors buy and sell gold over the counter (OTC) via exchange-traded funds, futures and options, warrants, gold accounts, gold accumulation plans, gold certificates, mining company stocks, gold-oriented funds, and on and on. Financial markets are always in search of new opportunities, and the gold market is no different. The effect on attempts to increase accountability in the supply chain is profound, as this complexity severely limits efforts to track and trace gold from mine to buyer.

So who is buying all these products? Investing in gold has indeed become mainstream, with individuals, pension funds, sovereign wealth funds, and central banks all getting in on the act. In fact, with countless new intermediaries, and the continued financialisation of markets, many people are unwittingly investing in gold through their pension funds and registered retirement savings plans. And to add further complexity to an already complex picture, these transactions take place in a multiplicity of exchanges around the world. The good news is that more than 90 per cent of global trading volumes takes place in London, New York and Shanghai.[10] The bad news is that these transactions remain complex and discreet.

The London OTC market is the largest in the world, accounts for an estimated 70 per cent of trades worldwide, and has traditionally set the price for gold through its method of 'discovery' taking place twice a day.[11] It is administered by the London Bullion Market Association, which is affiliated with the Bank of England. This is where the big players meet to swap gold. Central bankers, miners, refiners, fabricators and funds all come together to trade directly with one another. It is a popular way to trade gold, as, among other things, it offers confidentiality to the principal traders.[12]

When the US Congress repealed the Gold Reserve Act of 1934, which prohibited the private ownership of gold in the US, New York and Chicago were set to become the largest gold futures and options exchanges in the world.[13] In 2006, the NYMEX was purchased by the Chicago Mercantile Exchange (CME Group) and merged with COMEX. With almost half a million transactions a day, COMEX has become a global powerhouse in gold derivatives. These futures and options are linked to physical gold, but the majority of transactions taking place do not end in the delivery of physical gold bars.

While both the London and US commodities markets remain the bedrock for business in Asia, there is also a new game in town for Asian investors. The People's Bank of China established the Shanghai Gold Exchange (SGE) in 2002. Later in the chapter, we will return to the SGE, as well as the more recently established Shanghai Futures Exchange (SHFE), which have combined to put the Chinese gold market on the map. The next section looks first at the growing popularity of gold, especially in Asia, and the ways in which the flow of gold once again reflects and reinforces power shifts in the global political economy.

Emerging power in supply and demand

2018 was a big year for gold. Central banks across the world embarked on the largest buying spree of the commodity for almost half a century. This spree was not led by the US or the EU, or even by China, but by Russia, Turkey and Kazakhstan.[14] Russia alone bought 274 tonnes, about 42 per cent of all the gold bought by countries that year. That is the largest net purchase on record.[15] What can explain such a bold acquisition of the safest of safe assets?

There is little doubt that many conspiracy theorists in the darker corners of the Internet would be quick to jump to conclusions. The allegations against the Russian regime are well known: Russia may be deliberately stoking political instability, everywhere from alleged interference in the US elections and the Brexit referendum to undermining democracy in Europe and the Middle East. Is it possible that Russia is anticipating more instability of its own making, and so amassing gold to protect its financial reserves? There may be a less convoluted yet more powerful explanation.

To understand what is really going on, we first need to take stock of recent developments in Siberia. It is perhaps ironic how the great resource rushes that have shaped history often take place far from population centres, at the edge of the map. Such is the case here, where one of the largest gold mines in history will soon break ground, in the remote eastern Siberian steppe, near the border with Mongolia.

The Kluchevskoye Gold Mining Project, located in the Chita region of Russia, is notable not only for its physical size. The preproduction investment alone is US$500 million, and the planned open pit mine will be gigantic when operational, producing approximately 6.5 tonnes of gold per year. Yet its true significance lies in who is behind the establishment of the mine.

This project is the first true multilateral public–private partnership in a gold mine. Public–private partnerships are infrastructure investment models that involve both government and private-sector investment. They are now common practice but rarely involve more than one country as an investor. This project has five: India, China, Russia, Brazil and South Africa. This sort of international partnership on a resource project is rare indeed. It also marks a global shift in power away from the West and underlines an idea we have emphasised throughout this book: gold is a global commodity, and, by tracing the streams and currents of the gold supply, we can glimpse the flow of power through history.

All five investor states in Kluchevskoye are members of the BRICS club of nations. A British banker and economist, Jim O'Neill, first coined the term BRIC – an acronym for Brazil, Russia, India and China – in 2001. The term, and his arguments about the BRIC nations, made O'Neill one of the more celebrated economists in London in the 2000s. His name seemed to be everywhere. In 2001, when he published the paper for which he will forever be known, entitled 'The world needs better economic BRICs', O'Neill had just become head of research at Goldman Sachs.

What was initially penned as a report for investors soon became an economic and political alliance. These countries – Brazil, Russia, India and China (South Africa was not yet included) – were drawn together by O'Neill as the rapidly emerging economic powers, representing exciting new investment opportunities for the bank's clients. Of course, these four countries did not mind being associated with one another, since new investment was always welcome. And so the term was willed into existence and, by 2006, the group of four had institutionalised BRICs as a political reality through various conferences and institutions. BRICs became BRICS in 2010, when South Africa joined the group to round out the regional representation.

The BRICS now account for almost half the world's population (c. 40 per cent), over half the world's economic growth since 2009 (c. 55 per cent) and around a quarter of the world's GDP (c. 25 per cent). And this shift in the global political economy goes even beyond the BRICS. For example, the GDP of the so-called E7 – emerging economies (China, India, Russia, Brazil, Indonesia, Mexico, Turkey) is about to surpass the GDP of the long established G7 – the group of seven industrialised economies (US, Japan, Germany, France, Italy, UK, Canada). While the GFC of 2007–8 slowed the global economy overall, it seems

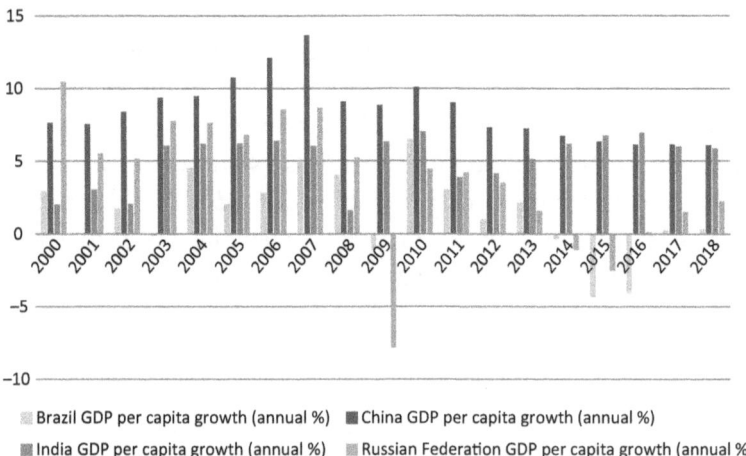

Figure 5.1   GDP growth per capita (annual %)
Source: World Bank, 2019, https://data.worldbank.org/.

to have only accelerated the shift in power from West to East by hitting the rich Western countries hardest, as they were more exposed to the problematic financial markets at the time.[16]

As debt continues to grow in the G7 countries, financial reserves are piling up in emerging economies. As noted already, those reserves include a sizable stockpile of gold. Russia, Turkey and Kazakhstan have not been alone in buttressing their gold reserves. The People's Bank of China has also been aggressively buying gold in recent months. Taken together, this constitutes a sea change in gold purchasing. For some time, it seemed central banks had lost their appetite for the precious metal, but, since the GFC, sales to governments are once again booming. Yet, this time around, governments in non-Western and emerging economies are leading the shopping spree. This, along with consumer demand, has helped prop up the gold price for the last decade.

Certainly, the instability in global markets and governance systems since 2008 can account for some of this. The price of gold, seen as a safe asset, runs counter-cyclical to global markets and so gold investors do especially well in uncertain times. But the real story of the boom in gold in recent years is the story of the BRICS.

Originally, the BRICS was a group of countries that an investment banker saw as a good opportunity for Goldman Sachs and its clients. But it does not take much imagination to see there were financial incentives for these countries to support this imagined community of emerging economies. For them, the idea of the BRICS became a political and economic opportunity. Thus, leaders in these countries embraced the grouping and used this convenient bit of branding to promote their own respective countries but also to advocate for the role of emerging countries in the global economy and global affairs.

This is not to say that it is, or ever was, a homogeneous group. In many ways, BRICS represents a group of very different states across most metrics, including their respective political institutions, issues of concern, paths to economic growth, and economic power. For example, China and Russia have authoritarian political systems. They are established global powers and have been for some time. Their pole positioning in issues of global security is enshrined in their seats on the United Nations Security Council (UNSC), as two of only five permanent members. In contrast, India, Brazil and South Africa are democracies, committed to the reform of the UNSC to reflect these fresh shifts in global power and, until recently at least, have shown an openness to discussing human rights and generally more progressive politics than the former. Another dimension of divergence among the BRICS can be seen in the structure of their economies. Brazil, Russia and

South Africa, for example, have driven their growth largely through resource extraction, while India has been focused on services and China on manufacturing. In terms of economic power, China's economy is bigger than those of the other four combined.

Despite these glaring differences, there are also ample similarities. This is especially true when thinking through the economic development experience of the trio of Brazil, China and India. All three states came from a leftist background, embracing state-led development and a socialist agenda (albeit with very different iterations, of course). In opening up to global markets, they all pursued some form of 'gradualism' instead of the 'shock' exposure famously, and in many cases tragically, experienced by the Russian economy following the collapse of the Soviet Empire. Gradualism – as the name implies – meant slowly shifting the economy to one that was more 'open' or laissez-faire. Each country has since developed and maintained a unique formula for mixing state intervention and economic openness. Their foreign policy positions also have some general similarities, as successive leaders in each have shown broad support for increasing respect for international sovereignty, commitments to multilateralism, and a desire to play a larger role in multilateral institutions.

These dramatic shifts in power and various positions on policy notwithstanding, the BRICS have shown little collective desire for anything resembling revolutionary change in the global political economy. And why should they? They have benefited greatly from the status quo. At least those who are well off in these emerging powers have done very well indeed. But simply the success of the BRICS has offered alternative models of economic development that have undercut prevailing wisdom in the major financial institutions (e.g. the World Bank, the IMF), development agencies (e.g. the UK Department for International Development, USAID), and corridors of power within developing and developed countries alike.

To many scholars and pundits, the rise of the BRICS signals a 'post-Washington consensus', a shift from economic policies that, until recently, were centred on American and European models. To many, the GFC further signalled the death knell of the neo-liberal model. The 'expertise' of the Western developed countries is no longer taken as given. Now there is more money and there are more models available for developing countries to draw upon for investment and advice. This increases the bargaining power of poor countries, both as aid recipients and as trading partners. It is clear – sometimes for better and sometimes for worse – that the idea of a 'strong state' is back in vogue, and state-structured development of industries and infrastructure along with it.

The emerging powers are also asserting their economic leverage through alliances and global institutions, as well as by forming new institutions altogether. This started with the creation of the so-called BRICS Bank (officially called the New Development Bank) and the Asian Infrastructure Development Bank, both set up to offer alternatives to the Washington-based development and financial institutions, namely the World Bank and IMF. This power shift is also playing out, and reflected, in the gold market.

BRICS and gold

Let's return to the Kluchevskoye Gold Mining Project in Siberia. In one sense, it is still stunning that five of the world's fastest growing economies are cooperating on this project. Yet, within the context of BRICS, the complex multilateralism at work here is less surprising. As power shifts away from the West, the gold market shifts too.

Ivor Ichikowitz, chairman of TransAfrica Capital, an investor in the Kluchevskoye project, has declared: 'This project marks a critical step in the evolution of BRICS, it is one of the first mega projects to be developed under the auspices of the BRICS collective.'[17] The initiative was spearheaded by India's SUN Gold Ltd and its chairman, Nand Khemka, who also recognises the significance of the project: 'This is BRICS 2.0. It is a logical extension of complementary strengths, helping to create more flexibility and innovation in the structure of transactions between members of the BRICS community. This is a winning formula.'[18] Cooperation on such projects offers a strikingly tangible example of the ways in which BRICS states continue to transform Jim O'Neill's acronym into reality. But, there is something that is potentially even more transformative happening in the global gold market.

The command centre for global gold is being steered eastwards, and it is again the BRICS countries at the helm. This is being signalled through the introduction of the BRICS single gold trading system – a gold trading system being built explicitly to counter the historical dominance of London. With intentions first surfacing in 2016, there has been swift movement to connect the Shanghai and Moscow gold trading centres, with aspirations not only to increase gold trading among the BRICS but also to introduce new gold pricing benchmarks. This makes a lot of sense, given that four of the five BRICS nations are top gold producers, and the one that is not, India, is one of the world's top consumers of the precious metal (again, along with China and Russia). With all of these countries being so heavily involved in the physical gold market, it seems strange for London or Geneva to remain their major trading hub. In fact, Sergey Shvetsov, the first deputy chairman of the Bank of Russia, has downplayed the continued significance of this traditional order, calling the London and Swiss gold trading operations less relevant in today's market.[19] In addition to making gold trading markets truly international, some analysts have suggested that one of the most noteworthy changes introduced through this shift will be the plan to base the gold price on physical gold assets and trade instead of the paper discovery (i.e. using OTC and derivatives markets to find the price), as has been the norm in the London and New York exchanges.[20]

Each individual country in the BRICS plays a significant role in the global gold market. Russia, for example, is the third largest gold producer in the world, behind only China and Australia. Having produced 297.3 tonnes of gold in 2018, the Russian Federation accounts for 14 per cent of total global production.[21] Russia also holds the third largest gold reserves worldwide, at 5.3 per cent of the global total, behind only

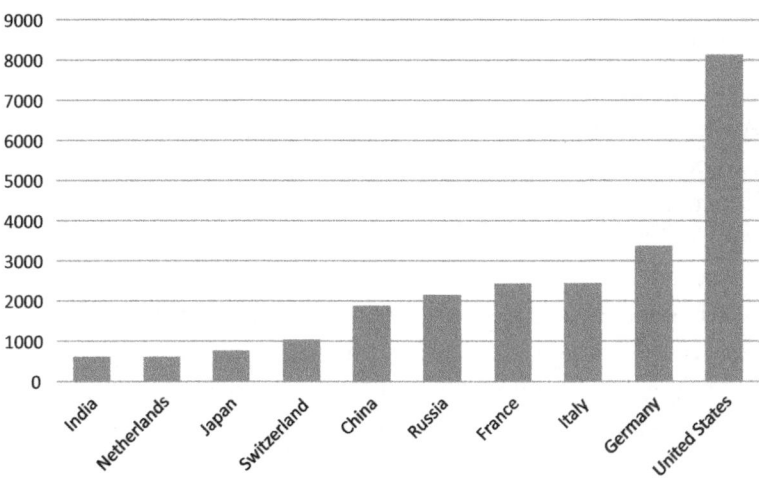

Figure 5.2   Official gold holdings of top ten countries, 2019 (tonnes)

Source: Heeb, G., The 10 countries with the biggest piles of gold, *Markets Insider*, 2019, https://markets.businessinsider.com/commodities/news/gold-countries-that-hold-largest-reserves-2019-4-1028128947#9-netherlands2 (based on data from World Gold Council and IMF).

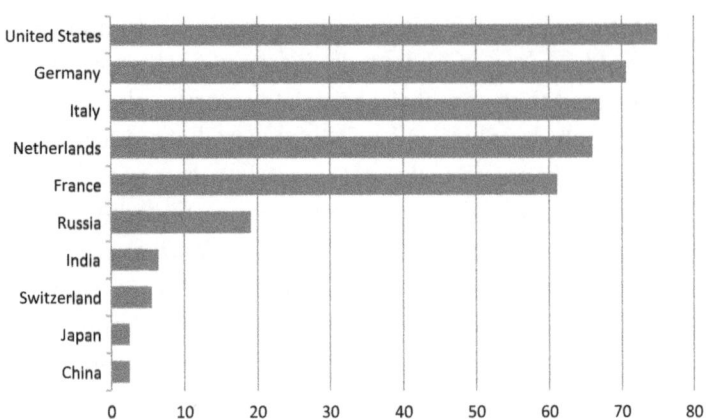

Figure 5.3   Foreign reserves held in gold of top ten countries, 2019 (%)

Source: Heeb, G., The 10 countries with the biggest piles of gold, *Markets Insider*, 2019, https://markets.businessinsider.com/commodities/news/gold-countries-that-hold-largest-reserves-2019-4-1028128947#9-netherlands2 (based on data from World Gold Council and IMF).

Australia and South Africa in this metric.[22] As touched upon earlier, the Russian state has been a major buyer in the bullion market and accounts for over 9 per cent of the official gold holdings worldwide, behind the US, Germany, Italy and France.[23]

When it comes to gold holdings as a percentage of all foreign reserves – a rough indicator of the value a country places on holding gold as opposed to other assets (at least historically) – we see roughly the same picture among the top ten gold holding countries, with only the Netherlands bumping the trend with its substantial hoard of gold.[24]

Brazil is also a mining nation. While the country gave birth to one of the largest mining companies around, Vale S.A., Brazil is better known for the low-tech, small-scale gold mining wreaking havoc on the Amazon rainforest and its inhabitants.

Historically, the Amazon gold rush drove the colonisation of the country and the enslavement of hundreds of thousands of people to work in the mines. The rich and dark history of gold mining in what is now Brazil has been well documented elsewhere, but suffice it to say that the Amazon gold rush has continued, with ebbs and flows, since the seventeenth century. Brazil falls just outside of the top ten producers but remains firmly within the top ten in terms of known gold reserves. With the price of gold reaching new heights, there is little reason to predict anything but a continuation of gold mining in Brazil for the foreseeable future.

South Africa has a long and shadowy mining history. For about a century, it was the largest gold producer in the world. Right up until China overtook it in production in 2007, South Africa maintained its dominance in the mining market established during the colonial era. But, since these dizzying heights, production has dropped by around 50 per cent or more. This rapid decline has taken place in only a couple of decades – a combination of rising production costs as a result of depleted stocks and higher input costs.[25] Despite the decline, South Africa still boasts the second largest gold reserves in the world and maintains a top-ten spot in gold production.

This leads us to China and India. China is the largest producer of gold in the world. India produces very little. But India is one of the largest consumers of gold. It was the number one consumer of gold until very recently when it lost top spot to China. But, together, these are two extremely significant markets that impact the political economy of gold. The combined demand from India and China has increased by 71 per cent in the last decade,[26] with China's demand for gold having more than doubled in just a few years.[27] The overall growth in both markets is due to a combination of cultural drivers and the rise of the middle class, the latter of which is of course intimately linked to the astonishing growth rates discussed earlier. But each country's gold market, and their respective roles in the global market, is uniquely interesting and impactful. The rise of these markets will have huge implications for the ways in which the gold market operates and, perhaps especially, for attempts to regulate it.

The Chinese gold market

China has the largest gold market in the world. In terms of extraction, its output has more than doubled in recent decades, and it now more than doubles the output of Australia or Russia, which are in second and third place, respectively. The impact of Chinese production on global markets is somewhat tempered by the fact that most Chinese-mined gold is consumed domestically. This gives us a pretty clear picture of the country's consumer appetite for gold. This is driven by both the desire for gold jewellery and a large and increasing appetite for gold as an investment asset. But, as with most developments in China, the state has carved out a role for itself.

Incentivised by this rising demand, the Chinese government redoubled its efforts to nurture and steer the gold market. Much of this has been done through partnerships – like the BRICS project described above – and through mergers and acquisitions. These strategies have been implemented at both ends of the supply chain and the stages in between. Now there is a significant Chinese presence all along the gold supply chain.

The Chinese mining sector

As discussed in chapter 2, mining is a core component of China's grand 'Belt and Road Initiative', the country's global development strategy. Mining is also a key element of reducing dependency on foreign and especially Western powers. China has aggressively engaged in expanding its activities in all things mining and all things gold. This has clearly been successful, since the country has very quickly become the world's largest gold producer, while also becoming one of the largest gold refiners. Given the strategic importance of metals mining to China's growth strategy, it is difficult to imagine the government putting the brakes on its expanding contribution to gold production and trade – or indeed passing regulation that might dampen it. In fact, the evidence suggests the opposite is much more likely to happen.

While China is still mostly focused on domestic production, in chapter 2 we explored how Chinese mining companies have expanded their investments rapidly in Africa, Latin America and elsewhere. This matters because many of these companies have clearly lacked a commitment to responsible mining, have maintained poor connections to the places in which they do business, and have influenced mining regulation with mixed results. So the fact that we are witnessing the rise of large and expanding Chinese companies and partnerships operating worldwide could be significant in terms of industry norms and practice.

We have also seen how complex the mining industry can be. This complex landscape is in constant flux. So, although the Chinese state has a particularly robust relationship with Chinese companies, attaching national labels to companies is an increasingly fuzzy affair, as shifting partnerships, mergers and acquisitions in the industry make ownership structures complex. Nevertheless, the big conglomerate for China is China National Gold Group Corporation (CNGGC). It is centrally owned by the state and is the largest gold producer in China, with controlling shares in other large gold mining entities such as Zhonghi Gold, which was the first publicly listed gold mining company in the country. CNGGC is not only involved in extraction of gold but is also the parent company of Gold Jewelry Corporation Ltd, which in turn owns the large China Gold brand. Other large Chinese mining companies of note are Shandong Gold (the company that is deepening its partnership with Canada's Barrick Gold) and the Zijin Mining Group, but there are many others. What most of these companies have in common is that they engage in some mix of domestic and overseas exploration and development and are listed on the Shanghai Stock Exchange.

These companies are leading the growth in Chinese investment in mining projects abroad. The Chinese government has actively encouraged this of both the private and state-owned companies. So companies such as China Gold International Resources is headquartered in Vancouver, Canada, and listed on the Toronto Stock Exchange (TSX), but it is partially owned by CNGGC as its main overseas vehicle.[28] While much of the company's expansion has been on the African continent, CNGGC made news when, on 29 March 2013, eighty-three workers were buried alive at their exploration-site in Tibet after the company had, allegedly, ignored multiple complaints and concerns voiced by the local community and stakeholders.[29]

We have also seen increasing foreign investment in Chinese gold mining companies and mines. This is where it starts to get really complicated. For example, one such investor is Jinshan Gold Mines Inc., located in Vancouver. Its biggest project is the Chang Shan Hao Mine, operating out of Inner Mongolia (i.e. within China). The Chang Shan Hao Mine is one of China's largest gold mines being run by a foreign company. But this Canadian company is actually in large part owned by Chinese interests: CNGGC bought 42 per cent of the business from Ivanhoe Mines (another Canadian company located in Vancouver) in 2008, giving it a majority share. Likewise, Australia's Sino Gold Mining Ltd (in partnership with South African Gold Fields Ltd) operates the Jinfeng Gold Mine, which was at one point the largest foreign investment in China's mining industry and the first foreign mining company to operate there. But, in 2016, CNGGC bought an 82 per cent stake from Eldorado Gold Corp. (a Canadian company), after it had previously acquired Sino Gold in 2009. Such moves reflect the complexity of a global industry that, at first glance, seems tasked with a fairly simple mandate: to acquire land, dig up gold and sell it. The reality is not so simple. The constantly shifting landscape, driven by mergers and acquisitions, demonstrates that transactions go well beyond discovering and extracting gold; rather, it further reflects the financialisation of the industry and the high-stakes plays that transcend national borders and economies.

The Chinese financial sector and gold investment
The Chinese government has increased activity in gold markets. Chinese actors are making an impact all along the supply chain, displacing the traditional actors and locations that have dominated the trade. This is perhaps nowhere more apparent than in the financial markets for gold.[30]

The massive, albeit gradual, market liberalisation taking place in China has created huge opportunities for both Chinese investors and potential foreign investors in China. New products and prospects in and around gold are no exception. As the largest producer and consumer of gold worldwide, it is little surprise that China has taken steps to increase its influence in gold markets.

Together, the Shanghai Gold Exchange (SGE) and the Shanghai Futures Exchange (SHFE) form the foundation of the Chinese gold market. This new powerhouse has come into being rather rapidly. The SGE was established in 2002. In 2004, the Chinese government permitted individuals to invest in gold, creating the basis for a now booming retail investment market. In 2005, the Industrial and Commercial Bank of China and the SGE partnered up to launch the Jinhangjia, as a spot trading product for private investors. In 2006, CNGGC, with support from the World Gold Council in London, launched the China Gold Investment Bar, a bullion product traded at SGE listed prices, with a small margin for domestic investors.[31] In 2008, the SHFE was created to introduce the 'gold future', which was open to retail investors, meeting the increasing demand from domestic investors and allowing companies to hedge against market fluctuations and downturns. Most recently, in 2016, the SGE launched the Shanghai Gold Price benchmark, which made China join the ranks of the price setters in London and New York. In making these bold moves, the Chinese government has created a gold market that it hopes will one day rival those traditional trading centres; in so doing, it continues the pull of gold from West to East.

The Indian gold market

India has always played a large role in the global gold market and, like China, is expanding its presence. But, in contrast to China, India has not yet carved out a significant role in gold production. However, Indian markets are significant in driving demand from the consumer end of the supply chain.

Gold is deeply embedded in Indian culture and society. This, combined with the monumental impact of India's consumer demand, has resulted in a gold market that ebbs and flows with the Indian cultural calendar. For example, the Indian wedding season generates a demand surge felt in gold markets around the world. Consumer market research conducted by TNS, on behalf of the World Gold Council, found that Indian weddings accounted for 24 per cent of gold purchases, followed by birthdays at 15 per cent and religious festivals at 12 per cent. In addition, the study found that Indian gold purchases align with the agricultural calendar, as around two-thirds of the Indian population participates in the rural economy. All said, 72 per cent of the respondents to the survey reported owning fine gold jewellery, with 55 per cent having bought some in the previous twelve months, and 51 per cent planning to buy more in the following twelve months.[32]

India has one of the fastest growing economies in the world, with growth rates consistently between 6 and 7 per cent, according to the IMF and World Bank. Amazingly, the growth in the gold jewellery market has been keeping pace, and even overtaking these impressive figures.[33] Clearly linked, income growth is the most significant driver of rising demand for gold jewellery. While the current market is slightly smaller than China's, which only recently overtook India as the largest consumer market for gold jewellery, the two will be battling for top spot for some time. This is especially apparent when one considers India's demographics – almost half the population is under twenty-five years old – and the projected growth in production and consumption this will bring in the coming years.

This large and growing gold market is undergoing some equally large changes. Traditionally an informal and loosely organised marketplace, it is quickly becoming reorganised in two ways, both of which will have enormous ramifications for buyers and sellers of gold worldwide. First, larger, branded jewellers are entering a market that has been dominated traditionally by small, informal and family-run gold dealers. Second, the global movement for increased transparency in supply chains has arrived in India, and this will impact the organisation of the gold market, including finance, in significant ways.[34]

The Indian jewellery market: formalisation and consolidation
When in India, one notices the connection to gold immediately. It is everywhere. In family photos, on billboards and in shops, gold is omnipresent in big cities and small towns alike. Buying and selling gold is a deeply ingrained practice in the economy, a truly familiar, even informal, transaction. Most people relay similar stories of their experience with gold purchasing. Their families have tended to buy gold from the same person or family-run business, or they are sometimes put in touch with another through friends and family. They would not normally shop in large jewellery stores or look for particular brands. On the contrary, they would bring their designs, and often their gold, to their family dealer, who would make it for them or arrange for it to be made. Transactions are made in cash and rarely recorded. Gold is gifted at most significant events and, when necessary, is used as collateral for loans big and small. Every family has some. Thus, gold is both a gift and an heirloom, representing liquidity and security. These small, family-run, informal transactions add up to around three-quarters of the US$45 billion a year gold industry in India. But the industry is changing.

Shifts in demographics and policies can explain many of the changes. As young people increasingly move further from home and into urban centres, branded jewellers are becoming more common. As such, many individuals will not have the personal connections to assure a fair deal in the informal markets. Brands offer a semblance of accountability for these consumers when it comes to purity. As many of the younger generation move to online shopping, smaller jewellers are expected to feel even more of a pinch. Industry analysts are expecting formalisation and consolidation to dominate the industry headlines for some time to come.[35]

As Bloomberg has extensively reported, industry formalisation and consolidation is being driven by Prime Minister

Modi's demonetisation drive. In an attempt to bring 'grey money' – money circulating through the informal economy and, therefore, able to avoid taxation – into the formal economy, Modi has undertaken a number of policies that impact the gold market. He has banned large-denomination notes, introduced proof of identity for large purchases, capped cash transactions, and introduced a uniform sales tax (GST). This GST is fixed at 3 per cent for gold, replacing a much more complex system that incentivised unrecorded transactions and made gold extremely difficult to track and trace.[36]

As Chirag Sheth, a London gold analyst familiar with the Indian market, put it: 'Bigger jewellers have deeper pockets, they have larger shops, better designs and better margins. It is very difficult for a smaller guy to compete.'[37] Nowhere is this industry consolidation more evident than with Rajesh Exports, the company started by Rajesh Mehta, now a billionaire. He and his brother began the business in the late 1980s by manufacturing gold jewellery out of their garage. They expanded to retail and are now extending their presence all along the gold supply chain. In the process, they are signalling a changing of the guard in the gold market. In 2015, for example, their company purchased the largest gold refiner in the world, the Swiss company Valcambi. Since then, it has been buying up mining companies in an attempt to secure its supply of gold while continuing to expand its retail brand, SHUBH Jewellers. The company owns mines across the globe, is increasingly vertically integrated, and markets itself as increasing transparency to the industry, selling at the 'real gold rate'. It all seems to be working, too. At the time of writing, the Rajesh Mehta group of companies processes approximately 35 per cent of gold produced in the world and has sales of over US$24 billion per year, making it one of only three companies from the Indian private sector to make it onto the Fortune 500 list.[38]

Even though large companies such as Rajesh have seen the writing on the wall, and have taken steps to secure their future supply of gold in light of increasing Asian demand, mine production in India remains minimal. This, of course, has to do with a relative lack of (known) gold deposits on the subcontinent. The best option remains buying mines abroad to achieve the desired security. But one area in which India is expanding is in refining – and for the same reasons. There are extensive new imports of unrefined gold coming in, from Ghana, the US and now Peru.[39] A new gold production hub is emerging.

Indian finance and gold: monetisation, loans and investment
Modi's government is also trying to bring all the gold floating around India into the formal financial system, so that it is available for investment. This makes perfect sense when one considers there is an estimated US$800 billion worth of gold in private households. It is not the first time the Indian state has tried this tactic, though. In the 1990s, the Indian government tried to lure idle gold out of households and into the financial system through the Gold Deposit Scheme. The goal was to put this gold to productive use by creating an incentive for individuals and families to lend it to the government. Clients could now deposit their physical gold – in the form of bars, coins or jewellery – and collect interest on it, with tax exemptions for those who took advantage of the scheme. But, even with these incentives in place, deposits remained meagre. This has been blamed on the relatively low use of banks among Indian households and the relatively high minimum deposit of 500 grams. But the Revamped Gold Deposit Scheme has lowered this minimum deposit from 500 grams to 30 grams, which may show better results.

Yet gold does already play a significant role in the Indian financial system. Its 'invisibility' is largely due to the fact that many gold transactions are informal. Using gold as collateral is common practice, giving rise to the largely informal economy of gold buyers and sellers discussed above. Many of these are basically pawnbrokers, but banks and formal gold loan companies have been increasing their share of the market.[40] This practice has been going on for a long time and is widespread across India. The interest rates tend to be competitive, and it has been a popular option for people who need short-term loans to cover short-term costs. According to research conducted by the World Gold Council, only about 68 per cent of Indians use banks, which is a much lower usage rate than in other countries. Perhaps it should come as no surprise, then, that the Indian market for exchange-traded funds and similar gold-backed financial instruments is relatively small.

Shifting implications for responsible gold?

These big global shifts in gold production and consumption are not the underlying cause of the tipping balance of power from West to East, but they are reflecting and reinforcing the realignment of power. How do these shifts in the gold market impact the options moving forward in terms of making gold work better for those most affected by its production and consumption? We have already engaged in some of the implications of the increasing Chinese presence in Africa and the substantial debates that surround it. However, there are similar issues to consider at the consumer end of the chain.

In its campaign for responsible jewellery, Human Rights Watch has included a few Indian jewellers in its ranking of major retailers on responsible sourcing. The three Indian companies it includes – Kalyan, TBZ Ltd and Tanishq – all scored very poorly. In fact, they were the lowest ranked out of the thirteen companies considered worldwide. Tanishq scored the lowest, as 'very weak', while Kalyan and TBZ Ltd scored 'no ranking', for not providing information to the campaign to rank them at all. These latter two were joined only by Rolex, which has notoriously decided not to engage in similar exercises and similar campaigns in the past, as we touched on in chapter 4.[41]

To date, there is little evidence that companies in the two largest gold jewellery markets – China and India – have taken any steps towards responsible sourcing. This is partly because campaigns have not targeted these markets, partly because they have only recently shifted to brands that might be impacted by such pressure, and partly because there has been little consumer demand for this responsibility.[42] This has raised more than a little concern about relying on jewellers – and the campaigns that target them – to drive positive change through the industry. Such concerns about 'rogue jewellers' parallels the types of considerations raised by Western development agencies when the BRICS countries, especially China, began providing vast sums of investment capital to developing countries, rivalling the money flowing from the West, but without any conditions attached in terms of governance priorities or human rights.[43]

This, of course, was seen as potentially diluting the efforts of large Western development agencies to leverage their funds to steer government policy in directions they considered desirable. While the debates around the actual impact of BRICS investment in developing countries will continue, as will debates around the appropriateness of conditional investment and aid from the West, there is little doubt that the combined demand for gold from India and China will severely limit any market leverage activists were hoping to get from the big Western brands of jewellery. As discussed in chapter 4, while activists have managed to garner only very limited leverage through brands in the US market, the ability to leverage these Asian markets, as they are currently structured, seems extremely slender indeed, even non-existent. Gold and gold jewellery are simply too culturally embedded, and the industry in India remains too fragmented. Moreover, consumers are simply unaware of the issues. Similar challenges face campaigners in China. While recent studies show some support for sustainability among Chinese consumers, including indications of a willingness to pay more for sustainably produced food and agricultural commodities,[44] the Chinese market for jewellery is based less on emotive marketing and is more closely linked to investment. Jewellery prices reflect weight and purity, with much smaller mark-ups for design and branding.[45] As such, the 1,143 tonnes of gold destined for the Indian and Chinese jewellery markets acts only as a safety valve for suppliers who might want to avoid scrutiny, dwarfing the 132.4 tonnes of gold headed to the US market that has been largely targeted by activists.[46]

Conclusion

At this point, it is difficult not to hear the echoes of 'get gold!' reverberating along the Belt and Road groundwork and, indeed, along the corridors of power in all the BRICS countries, now firmly established at the commanding heights of the global economy. The mercantilist scramble for 'specie', still clearly a strategic asset, appears alive and well. Likewise, the desire to establish a new centre for gold trading in the East, to counter the historical dominance of the West, makes it clear that gold maintains its close links with power. The more the gold market changes, the more we are reminded of what has stayed the same.

These recent transformations in financial flows and geopolitical shifts are making it increasingly difficult to regulate the gold industry. Faced with the growing complexity brought by the continuing financialisation of gold, it is clear that the predominant approaches for governing it are losing their leverage. It is becoming increasingly difficult to make the links between the impacts of gold mining and its producers and consumers, and even more challenging to create incentives for a critical mass of producers and consumers to act responsibly when these links are made. When we consider that over a quarter of all gold is accounted for by investment markets – and this rises to almost a half of all gold demand if one includes central bank buying – the ability for activists to force significant changes in global practices by leveraging the end-use brands associated with consumer goods in Western markets seems unlikely.

In short, complexity, opacity and culture combine to dilute the potential leverage of activists by giving the sellers of gold (i.e. the miners and traders) many 'exit options' when it comes to finding buyers. As one activist readily admitted: you can always sell gold.[47] This appears truer than ever. Instead of forcing actors in the supply chain to change their practices, it seems that supply chain actors are managing the issues on their own terms and in accordance with their own market priorities. This will surely temper the rate of substantive change in industry practices, to say the least. In fact, prospects for effective gold governance may even be diminishing. In the final chapter, we review our analysis, assess the current predicament, and offer some suggestions for ways forward.

CHAPTER 6

Conclusion:
Refocusing for the Future of Gold

To borrow a phrase from the World Gold Council, gold is in many ways 'a commodity like no other'.[1] It has a long history and deep links to centres of power. It has driven empires and fuelled wars. It has shaped state development strategies and the qualities of development outcomes. And of course the communities in which gold is mined have felt these effects most acutely. Gold's impacts reverberate across resource-rich countries by shaping the social, economic and ecological environment. Indeed, gold's impact rings around the world through its role in financial markets and geopolitics alike.

It should by now be clear how difficult gold is to regulate, though many have tried. Current efforts to make gold production more environmentally and socially just, or at least more benign, have achieved mixed results. The governance landscape is extremely fragmented, and change has been incremental at best. Complexity remains a challenge, as does the distinct lack of transparency and the industry culture that values this secrecy.

Despite the many unique characteristics of gold and its governance, the arguments we have presented in this book also hold lessons for other global resources. For example, in chapter 2, we noted how the issues underlying the so-called resource curse have most often been associated with energy resources such as oil.[2] Equally, the various links being made between gold and conflict are shared with other 'conflict' resources, including coltan, diamonds and even timber.[3] The challenges faced by workers in terms of their personal health and the health of their communities will resonate across sites of extraction beyond gold. Likewise, the inequality that is manifest in the uneven distribution of both the risks and the benefits of global production are not exclusive to gold supply chains. Look no further than the multitude of Fairtrade initiatives for agricultural products to reveal the extent to which these issues are shared across sectors.

The ecological issues associated with the widespread use of cyanide and mercury are specific to gold mining. However, reconciling the mass consumption of a growing middle class, the business models of increasingly global corporations, and the ability to push the ecological costs of industrial activity far down its supply chain is a persistent problem that extends well beyond gold. Thus, while the combination of gold's history, its links to power, its material characteristics, the complexity and opacity of its supply chains, and the culture of the industry have created extraordinary governance challenges, some of the key issues we have identified in the political economy of gold will also extend to other resources. Other resource sectors will have experimented with similar strategies to tackle these problems and will be facing comparable future regulatory challenges as power shifts in the global political economy.

Indeed, many of the strategies to govern gold parallel those being pursued in the governance of other global resources. For example, the emergence of the consumer as an overt political agent is a trend repeated across resource supply chains. Spurred on by transnational activist networks, consumer buying power is being leveraged against irresponsible business practices in many industries. Business habitually responds through a mix of corporate social responsibility programmes, industry-wide initiatives, multi-stakeholder meetings and certification regimes.

The outcomes we have seen in the gold sector are, more or less, mirrored in the results that can be seen elsewhere: a complex and fragmented resource governance landscape.

This new reality can be interpreted as a positive 'pluralism' – an emerging tapestry of global governance that, if properly interlinked with public regulation, can result in comprehensive regulatory coverage.[4] The danger is that, if they are not complementary, these initiatives instead simply contribute to a proliferation of disparate initiatives that not only fail to govern effectively but also distract from and delay potentially more robust regulation. Because diverse governance mechanisms cannot be painted with the same brush, it remains important to differentiate between those that have been successful in protecting industry reputations and those that have been effective in actually addressing the underlying issues associated with resource production and consumption.

Likewise, emerging regulatory challenges in gold are also applicable to other commodity sectors. For example, financialisation has been a scourge to activists attempting to change practices of industrial agriculture.[5] As seen with gold, financialisation adds layers of complexity to an already complex supply chain, scuppering activist attempts to make links between market actors and the social, economic and ecological impacts of their market decisions. Financialisation also comes with an increasing dependency on financial markets and on the decision-making of financial intermediaries. While financial markets can supply much needed capital to grow industries, financial speculation can lead to price volatility and uncertainty, producing difficulties in budgeting for both governments and households.

As we have seen in stark detail throughout this book, surging prices can drive scrambles for gold. Such arrangements seem mainly to benefit investors with only short-term interests in the market, while those toiling at the bottom of global supply chains can feel the repercussions of these investment decisions for a very long time. As nebulous centres of financial power drift to the East, there will be implications for world trade, investment, development and governance for almost all resources. When we consider the prospects for social and environmental regulation in this context, many states remain ill-equipped to withstand such powerful forces, while the civil society tactics of the past will likely prove ineffective.

Certainly in the case of gold, the power that dominates the sector continues to tame any meaningful attempts at transformational change. There are numerous innovative initiatives that have attempted to address this power imbalance. Although many of these initiatives complement one another in productive ways, evidence of real change in practices remains thin. Patience could be preached, but we have also seen ample reason to believe that gold is becoming more, and not less, difficult to regulate. The story may be a dark one, but there are also glimmers of hope throughout. We found these in the initiatives of forward thinking states, brave activists and even proactive businesses. In the remainder of this final chapter, we draw inspiration from these as we reflect on the future of gold and search for a way forward.

Considering the future of gold

Perhaps the first question to ask is whether sustainable and responsible gold is even possible. History suggests it is unlikely. The history of gold instead conjures images of colonial conquest, a cowboy culture of lies and deceit, and the persistent exploitation of people and the planet. A gold find rarely makes the weak powerful. Rather, it is more likely that the powerful will swoop in to consolidate their wealth and their position.

Throughout this book, we have attempted to lay bare the stark realities that persist along the global gold supply chain. The debates in which we have engaged, the examples we have presented, and the stories we have told all help us understand the stakes involved.

For the miners working in the industry, especially those barely eking out a livelihood from small-scale gold mining, and for the communities affected by gold extraction, both negatively and positively, the stakes are very high indeed. But simply understanding the challenges and barriers is clearly not enough to make gold mining more equitable, more sustainable and more responsible. To achieve these goals, structural change is needed. Specifically, transformations in both the political economy and social relations related to the production and consumption of gold will first need to take place.

At the extreme end, some would advocate for the end of gold as an acceptable adornment, sending it off the way of fur or ivory. But the fact that gold is so deeply embedded in all elements of the global political economy, from micro to macro, suggests this is an unlikely outcome, whether one believes it desirable or not. In any case, gold itself is obviously not the problem. It is the historically entrenched social relations and contemporary power asymmetries that have dictated where, when and how to mine, and where and to whom the spoils flow. And these dynamics are within our control. Through political pressure and robust regulation, there are opportunities to make the gold industry work better for everyone. Looking forward, we now turn to one particular area where we believe such opportunities exist: the artisanal and small-scale gold mining (ASGM) sector.

ASGM as a driver of (sustainable) development

In our minds, the ASGM sector is an obvious place to focus first. Although large-scale, capital-intensive gold mining projects have long captured the imaginations of governments, policymakers and development professionals, ASGM is by far the largest employer at the point of extraction, providing a livelihood for tens of millions of individuals across the globe. Recent scholarship on artisanal and small-scale mining has increasingly recognised how the sector has the potential to safeguard livelihoods, alleviate poverty, and drive rural development at the local level.[6] If effectively managed, a supported ASGM sector could play an important role in contributing to almost all of the SDGs.

More specifically, these discussions have been couched in detailed analysis of how miners innovate in informal small-scale mining spaces and of the role that a formalised ASGM sector could play in supporting extractive-led development trajectories. A formalised sector, it has been argued, could directly address SDG 1 (no poverty), SDG 2 (end hunger), SDG 8 (decent work and economic growth) and SDG 10 (reduce inequality). Moreover, it could also promote better environmental management by addressing SDG 6 (clean water and sanitation for all), SDG 14 (life below water), SDG 15 (protect, restore and promote the sustainable use of terrestrial ecosystems and halt biodiversity loss) and SDG 12 (responsible consumption and production).

Central to ASGM's ability to foster entrepreneurial activity and support the SDGs is the recognition that the sector is situated at the heart of local people's diversified livelihood 'portfolios' across the developing world. Indeed, it is most often the case that individuals in mining communities engage in a range of different livelihood activities throughout the year, where mining remains the central non-farm income-generating activity. This positioning allows the sector to generate vital 'start-up' capital for upstream and downstream activities, offer jobs in employment-constrained economies and, in many cases, nourish smallholder agriculture. Critical scholars have argued that relationships between small-scale mining and the SDGs involve a dynamic process of transformation in rural societies. If the conditions are right, the process could help to foster a platform for wealth creation and opportunities to build sustainable and innovative economies. This could serve as a foundation for spawning entrepreneurship and catalysing sustainable economic linkages locally, both of which are important processes for attaining the SDGs.

Perhaps most significantly, the ASGM sector could be an effective vehicle for stimulating the growth of ancillary industries, even in situations where finance and capital investments are in short supply. Many mining communities across the developing world have increasingly diversified their economic bases, with recent growth in trading, simple manufacturing, services, and administrative activities. Such linkages are perhaps most evident in the innovative and entrepreneurial synergies that are often created between artisanal mining and the smallholder farming economy. Early work by Maconachie and Binns explored the mining-farming nexus in Sierra Leone.[7] The study focused on the interlocking nature of the agricultural and artisanal mining sectors and their tendency to 'dovetail'. In the case of Sierra Leone, analysis suggests that the increasing production of foodstuffs for mining-area markets has actually promoted changes in traditional food production systems, most notably a shift to the production of fruits and vegetables, as well as cash crops for export. This, in turn, has stimulated the growth of a large and buoyant group of itinerant traders who have been able to benefit from the linkages created between the farming and mining economies.[8]

In short, recent literature suggests that ASGM can contribute to sustainable rural development by providing job opportunities, increasing income generation and local purchasing power, stimulating local economic development, slowing urban migration, and facilitating technology transfers. Moreover, the strong degree of entrepreneurship present in mining communities can be a transformational driver, providing the bedrock for delivering the SDGs while simultaneously fuelling sustainable economic growth.

Within studies of sustainable development, entrepreneurship is frequently championed as a vehicle for empowerment and an enabler of economic growth, poverty alleviation and human development.[9] SDG 9 (industry, innovation and infrastructure) suggests that innovation is a major force for both economic growth and development as well as a crucial driver for job creation and livelihood stability, especially for young people and marginalised groups. This has fed directly into recent interest in gender and mining and the role that women assume in the informal small-scale mining sectors in developing countries, particularly with the current drive for the formalisation of these sectors.

For example, recent interviews with women gold panners in Sierra Leone revealed that their earnings from gold were being used to finance local agricultural businesses and trading ventures.[10] Several women we interviewed described how, with the income derived from gold panning, they were able to purchase a wide range of fresh foodstuffs from nearby villages, including cassava, aubergines, oranges, limes and mangoes, which they would then transport to the capital city, Freetown, to sell at much higher prices. Many of these rural entrepreneurs were well aware that they could make considerable profits through such trading endeavours.

Without doubt, the ASGM sector in Sierra Leone has a prominent gender dimension. Women dominate the sector. But the country's policy machinery currently in place has done little to help entrepreneurial women fully harness the benefits of gold resources. Sierra Leone has embraced SDG 5 (gender equality) in many of its rural development policies and programmes. And it is widely acknowledged that increased financial stability and independence for women are needed to challenge deep-seated gender norms, influence unequal power structures and promote women's rights. Yet more needs to be done to tackle these entrenched problems in the ASGM sector. For example, women engaged in artisanal gold mining should be empowered as concession holders, so that they can own the sites where mining takes place. Such a move would have ripple effects, facilitating improved agricultural productivity and food security, and alleviating rural poverty even further.

In Sierra Leone and elsewhere, women have creatively used the ability to move freely in the informal gold mining space to support their households and reinvest small earnings into other economic activities. As a first step, a proper appreciation of the benefits that ASGM yields for rural households is essential, as is a gender-sensitive ASGM formalisation programme that speaks to the SDGs. These gendered aspects of artisanal and small-scale mining have been explored, to a limited degree, in recent academic literature.[11] Most new policy frameworks for formalisation recognise the need to take on board women's empowerment and gender equity as a primary concern. However, much more research needs to be undertaken to inform the formalisation process in a bid to ensure that gender is placed at the centre of design and implementation.

Taking stock and moving forward

It seems almost ironic that our journey has taken us across the global political economy of gold, focusing on its complex supply chains and linkages to centres of geopolitical power and the commanding heights of financial markets, and yet we seem to have returned to the site of extraction to find answers. Indeed, it remains imperative to focus on mining practices on the ground. While it is certainly true that environmental and social issues associated with gold are not confined to the site of extraction, the most directly impactful issues are. Regulating this space remains in the purview of individual states, and so refocusing attention on the willingness and ability of states to regulate remains a priority. Given that mining companies seek access to land and access to capital in approximately equal measures, such state regulation will need to be reinforced in both host and home countries alike. Because of the deregulatory pressures that states face, this will necessarily be an on-going endeavour.

It is tempting to conclude with a rousing appeal for a return to strong regulation by the state. But, of course, we have seen again and again how the state is also implicated in gold's negative impacts. Similarly, the promise shown by many non-state and market-driven initiatives is alluring. The idea that they could be ratcheted up, scaled up and rolled out holds much appeal and offers some hope. Of course, it would be worth exploring and experimenting with the ways in which these initiatives could be linked more directly to public regulation, to give them more procedural legitimacy and more 'teeth'. If the goal is transformational change at the site of extraction, the trick will be to ensure that they indeed supplement and do not supplant robust legislation.

In frustration, activists continue to circumvent traditional policy routes because of the perceived failures of the state to adequately address the impacts of gold mining at the site of extraction. But, at this point, it appears that the pendulum may have swung too far towards top-down, or downstream driven, supply chain solutions. Not only are downstream supply chain initiatives not working, but they seem to be even less likely to work given the shifting realities of the industry. And not only are these strategies becoming less likely to work, they come with three additional and potentially dangerous shortcomings: (1) they too often fail to address the complex political realities at each location gold mining takes place; (2) they risk individualising responsibility for these issues, drawing attention from the behaviour of producers to that of consumers; and (3) they are building complacency through the illusion of solving the problems and, therefore, are potentially forestalling robust regulation. Again, for all of these reasons, we stress the importance of drawing the policy focus back to the site of extraction, particularly in 'informal spaces' such as the ASGM sector, where millions of livelihoods are at stake.

None of this is to say that downstream initiatives are unimportant. But, when evaluating them, or any governance mechanism for that matter, it is always imperative to understand who these initiatives really serve and, relatedly, what practices they actually seek to change. If these initiatives simply allow consumers to feel good about their purchases or, worse yet, allow companies to continue producing and trading irresponsibly, the regulation is simply not fit for purpose. In fact, in cases such as this, it may be a step backwards, as it facilitates 'business as usual' by constructing complacency through the illusion of change.

In drawing the book to a close, we still do not claim to have all the answers. Far from it. But our goal has been to offer a comprehensive, if complex, picture of the global political economy of gold as a starting point for evaluating what works, what does not work, and why. In doing so, we place ourselves in a better position to navigate the significant challenges that lie ahead.

Notes

Chapter 1 Introduction

1 Waszkis, H., *Mining in the Americas: Stories and History*. Cambridge: Woodhead, 1993.
2 Wyss, J., and Gurney, K., Dirty gold is the new cocaine in Colombia – and it's just as bloody, *Miami Herald*, 16 January 2018, www.miamiherald.com/news/nation-world/world/americas/colombia/article194188034.html.
3 For more on the state of Venezuelan mining in the Amazon and its implications for people and the planet, see Moloney, A., Sex trafficking 'staggering' in illegal Latin American gold mines: researchers, *Reuters*, 30 March 2016, www.reuters.com/article/us-latam-trafficking-mines-idUSKCN0WW21U; Pons, C., and Ramirez, M., How Venezuela turns its useless bank notes into gold, *Reuters*, 10 February 2019, www.reuters.com/article/us-venezuela-gold-insight-idUSKCN1PZ0BX; and Wyss and Gurney, Dirty gold is the new cocaine in Colombia.
4 For a better understanding of the complex relationship that has developed between coca and gold, including reinvestments across the commodity sectors, see Massé, F., and Le Billon, P., Gold mining in Colombia, post-war crime and the peace agreement with the FARC, *Third World Thematics: A TWQ Journal*, 3/1 (2018): 116–34.
5 Graham-Harrison, E., and C. Rangel, Venezuela's gold fever fuels gangs and insecurity: 'There will be anarchy', *The Guardian*, 8 June 2019, www.theguardian.com/world/2019/jun/08/venezuela-puerto-ordaz-gold-mines-armed-gangs.
6 Steinhauser, G., and Bariyo, N., How 7.4 tons of Venezuela's gold landed in Africa – and vanished, *Wall Street Journal*, 18 June 2019, www.wsj.com/articles/how-7-4-tons-of-venezuelas-gold-landed-in-a

fricaand-vanished-11560867792; and Laya, P., and Rosati, A., Venezuela has 20 tons of gold ready to ship, address unknown, *Bloomberg*, 30 January 2019, www.bloomberg.com/news/arti cles/2019-01-30/venezuela-has-20-tons-of-gold-ready-to-ship-desti nation-unknown.

7 The video of this panel and the full transcripts of the talk are available online on the Brookings Institution website, at www.brookings. edu/events/financial-tools-for-us-policy-towards-nicaragua-and-ven ezuela-a-conversation-with-treasury-assistant-secretary-marshall-bil lingslea/.

8 One additional angle to this particular tale of gold is worth telling here, and it involves a young Turkish gold trader by the name of Reza Zarrab. Zarrab was arrested in the US in 2016 and has since turned into a key witness in the prosecution of Mehmet Hakan Atilla, a high-profile banker with ties to Turkey's President Recep Tayyip Erdoğan. The US courts allege that Atilla ran the gold trading scheme that facilitated Iranian access to international markets between 2010 and 2015 while US sanctions were in place. What is even more intriguing, if as yet unclear, is that Donald Trump's personal lawyer, Rudy Giuliani, is representing Zarrab. It appears that the Trump administration has been paying close attention to the case, perhaps sensing an opportunity to forward its own ambitions. This interest was only heightened when Zarrab later implicated Erdoğan directly in the scheme. Various major media outlets have been following this story. For more information on the ways in which this saga has unfolded, see Bump, P., Turkey, Iran, gold, Giuliani and Trump: a guide to the case of Reza Zarrab, *Washington Post*, 10 October 2019, www.washingtonpost.com/ politics/2019/10/10/turkey-iran-gold-giuliani-trump-guide-case-reza-zarrab/; Durkee, A., Report: Trump asked Rex Tillerson to help scrap a criminal case against Giuliani's client, *Vanity Fair*, 10 October 2019, www.vanityfair.com/news/2019/10/trump-reza-zarrab-giuliani-turkey-erdogan; Wadhams, N., Mohsin, S., Baker, S., and Jacobs, J., Trump urged top aide to help Giuliani client facing DOJ charges, *Bloomberg*, 9 October 2019, www.bloomb erg.com/news/articles/2019-10-09/trump-urged-top-aide-to-help-giuliani-client-facing-doj-charges; Smith, D., Giuliani under scrutiny over dealings involving Turkey and Ukraine, *The Guardian*, 12 October 2019, www.theguardian.com/us-news/2019/oct/11/rudy-

giuliani-trump-oval-office-turkey-iran-prisoner-swap; BBC, Reza
Zarrab case: gold trader implicates Turkish President Erdogan,
BBC News, 1 December 2017, www.bbc.com/news/world-
europe-42189802.

CHAPTER 2 GOLD AND THE DISTORTIONS OF
DEVELOPMENT

1 Bernstein, P. L., *The Power of Gold: The History of an Obsession*.
Chichester: Wiley, 2000, p. 1.
2 UNDP, *Mapping Mining to the Sustainable Development Goals:
A Preliminary Atlas*. New York: United Nations Development
Programme, 2016.
3 Vanden, H. E., and Prevost, G., *Politics of Latin America: The
Power Game*. New York: Oxford University Press, 2002, p. 34.
4 Chandra, R., *Industrialization and Development in the Third
World*. London: Routledge, 2004, p. 22.
5 Viner, J., Power versus plenty as objectives of foreign policy in the
seventeenth and eighteenth centuries, *World Politics*, 1/1 (1948):
1–29.
6 Mun, T., *England's Treasure by Forraign Trade*. New York:
Macmillan, [1664] 1895.
7 Viner, Power versus plenty as objectives of foreign policy.
8 See Mountford, B. W., and Tuffnel, S., How gold rushes helped
make the modern world, *The Conversation*, 3 April 2018, http://
theconversation.com/how-gold-rushes-helped-make-the-modern-
world-91746.
9 Kindleberger, C., *The World in Depression, 1929–1939*. Berkeley:
University of California Press, 1973.
10 Simmons, B. A., *Who Adjusts? Domestic Sources of Foreign
Economic Policy during the Interwar Years*. Princeton, NJ:
Princeton University Press, 1997.
11 Triffin, R., *Gold and the Dollar Crisis*. Rev. edn, New Haven,
CT: Yale University Press, 1961; Helleiner, E., *States and the
Reemergence of Global Finance: From Bretton Woods to the 1990s*.
Ithaca, NY: Cornell University Press, 1996.
12 Gowa, J. S., *Closing the Gold Window: Domestic Politics and the
End of Bretton Woods*. Ithaca, NY: Cornell University Press, 1983.

13 We will explore the implications of the currently surging appetite for gold-backed financial instruments in chapter 5, where we argue that gold is only becoming even more difficult to regulate.

14 UNEP, *Building Capacity for Environmental Sustainability in Artisanal and Small Scale Mining in Africa*. Addis Ababa: United Nations Economic Commission for Africa, 2017.

15 See Telmer, K., and Viega, M., World emissions of mercury from artisanal and small-scale gold mining, in N. Pirrone and R. Mason (eds), *Mercury Fate and Transport in the Global Atmosphere: Emissions, Measurements and Models*. Dordrecht: Springer, 2009, pp. 131–72; and Pirrone, N., Cinnirella, S., Feng, X., Finkelman, R. B., Friedli, H. R., Leaner, J., Mason, R., Mukherjee, A. B., Stracher, G. B., Streets, D. G., and Telmer, K., Global mercury emissions to the atmosphere from anthropogenic and natural sources, *Atmospheric Chemistry and Physics*, 10 (2010): 5951–64.

16 Otto, J., Andrews, C., Cawood, F., Doggett, M., Guj, P., Stermole, F., Stermole, J., and Tilton, J., *Mining Royalties: A Global Study of Their Impact on Investors, Government, and Civil Society*. Washington, DC: World Bank, 2006; Bridge, G., Mapping the bonanza: geographies of mining investment in an era of neoliberal reform, *Professional Geographer*, 56/3 (2004): 406–21.

17 Smith, M., The impact of Mali's political problems on the gold industry, *Gold Investing News*, 5 December 2012, http://goldinvest ingnews.com/30155/mali-political-problems-gold-industry-coup-great-quest-metals-mining.html.

18 Bridge, G., Global production networks and the extractive sector: governing resource-based development, *Journal of Economic Geography*, 8 (2008): 389–419, here p. 390.

19 Ibid., p. 391.

20 Fanthorpe, R., and Gabelle, C., *Political Economy of Extractives: Governance in Sierra Leone*. Washington, DC: World Bank, 2013.

21 Ferguson, J., *Global Shadows: Africa in the Neoliberal World Order*. Durham, NC: Duke University Press, 2006.

22 See Wegenast, T., Strüver, G., Giesen, J., and Krauser, M., *At Africa's Expense? Disaggregating the Social Impact of Chinese Mining Operations*, GIGA Working Paper no. 308, 2017, www.giga-ham burg.de/en/system/files/publications/wp308_wegenast-struever-gies en-krauser.pdf.

23 See Gallagher, K., and Porzecanski, R., *China and the Latin*

America Commodities Boom: A Critical Assessment, Political Economy Research Institute Working Paper no. 192, 2009, https://scholarworks.umass.edu/cgi/viewcontent.cgi?article=1161&=&context=peri_workingpapers&=&sei-redir=1&referer=https%253A%252F%252Fscholar.google.com%252Fscholar%253Fhl%253Den%2526as_sdt%253D0%25252C5%2526q%253DKevin%252BGallagher%252Bgold%252Bmining%252Bin%252Bchina%2526btnG%253D#search=%22Kevin%20Gallagher%20gold%20mining%20china%22.

24 Moody, R., Extraction to destruction? Chinese policy and practice in mining and metals, *Mines and Communities*, 22 December 2007, www.minesandcommunities.org/article.php?a=8342.

25 See China's gold mining industry: a story of growth, World Gold Council, 18 October 2018, www.gold.org/goldhub/research/gold-investor/gold-investor-october-2018/chinas-gold-mining-industry-a-story-of-growth.

26 Chinese gold mining as a source of gold supply, *BullionStar*, c.2017, www.bullionstar.com/gold-university/chinese-gold-mining-as-a-source-of-gold-supply.

27 For example, reports suggest that, in 2017, China imported gold raw materials of 854,150 tonnes, with a value of US$1.7 billion, including the purchase of precious metal ore sands and concentrates from fifty-five regions and countries – nineteen of these countries are within the B&R initiative area. See China's gold mining industry: a story of growth.

28 Imahashi, R., China goes for gold with overseas mining projects, *Nikkei Asian Review*, 30 July 2018, https://asia.nikkei.com/Business/China-goes-for-gold-with-overseas-mining-projects.

29 Crawford, G., and Botchwey, G., *Conflict, Collusion and Corruption in Small-Scale Gold Mining in Ghana: Chinese Miners and the State*, Colloquium Paper no. 48, The Hague: International Institute of Social Sciences, 2016.

30 See, for example, Hilson, G., Hilson, A., and Adu-Darko, E., Chinese participation in Ghana's informal gold mining economy: drivers, implications and clarifications, *Journal of Rural Studies*, 34 (2019): 292–303; Tschakert, P., Shifting discourses of vilification and the taming of unruly mining landscapes in Ghana, *World Development*, 86 (2016): 123–32; and Crawford G., Agyeyomah C., and Mba A., Ghana – big man, big envelope, finish: Chinese corporate

exploitation in small-scale mining, in B. Engels and K. Dietz (eds), *Contested Extractivism, Society and the State: Struggles over Mining and Land*. London: Palgrave Macmillan, 2017.

31 See Crawford and Botchwey, *Conflict, Collusion and Corruption in Small-Scale Gold Mining in Ghana*.

32 Gonzalez-Vicente, R., China's engagement in South America and Africa's extractive sectors: new perspectives for resource curse theories, *Pacific Review*, 24/1 (2011): 65–87.

33 See Rostow, W. W., *The Stages of Economic Growth: A Non-Communist Manifesto*. Cambridge: Cambridge University Press, 1960.

34 See Sachs, J. D., and Warner, A. M., *Natural Resource Abundance and Economic Growth*, National Bureau of Economic Research (NBER) Working Paper no. 5398, 1995; Sachs and Warner, Sources of slow growth in African economies, *Journal of African Economies*, 6/3 (1997): 335–76.

35 For example, see Collier, P., and Hoeffler, A., On economic causes of civil war, *Oxford Economic Papers*, no. 50 (1998): 563–73; Collier and Hoeffler, Resource rents, governance, and conflict, *Journal of Conflict Resolution*, 49/4 (2005): 625–33.

36 Heller, T. C., African transitions and the resource curse: an alternative perspective, *Journal of the Institute of Economic Affairs*, 26/4 (2006): 24–33, here p. 25.

37 Pegg, S., Mining and poverty reduction: transforming rhetoric into reality, *Journal of Cleaner Production*, 14 (2006): 376–87.

38 Ross, M., What do we know about natural resources and civil war?, *Journal of Peace Research*, 41/3 (2004): 337–56.

39 Rosser, A., *The Political Economy of the Resource Curse: A Literature Survey*, Working Paper Series no. 268. Brighton: Institute of Development Studies, 2006.

40 Standing, A., and Hilson, G., *Distributing Mining Wealth to Communities in Ghana: Addressing Problems of Elite Capture and Political Corruption*, U4 no. 5. Bergen: Anti-Corruption Resource Centre, 2013, p. 5.

41 Ibid.

42 International Council on Mining & Metals, *Ghana Country Case Study, The Challenge of Mineral Wealth: Using Resource Endowments to Foster Sustainable Development*. London: ICMM, 2007.

43 Standing and Hilson, *Distributing Mining Wealth to Communities in Ghana.*

44 Hilson, G., Corporate social responsibility in the extractive industries: experiences from developing countries, *Resources Policy*, 37/2 (2012): 131–7, here p. 133.

45 See How the 20 tons of mine waste per gold ring figure was calculated, https://earthworks.org/cms/assets/uploads/archive/files/publications/20TonsMemo_FINAL.pdf.

46 Horowitz, L. S., Interpreting industry's impacts: micropolitical ecologies of divergent community responses, *Development and Change*, 42/6 (2011): 1379–91.

47 Veiga, M., and Baker, R., *Protocols for Environmental and Health Assessment of Mercury Released by Artisanal and Small-Scale Gold Miners.* Vienna: UNIDO Global Mercury Project, 2004.

48 See Hinton, J., Veiga, M., and Beinhoff, C., Women, mercury and artisanal gold mining: risk communication and mitigation, *Journal de Physique IV (Proceedings)*, 107 (2003): 617–20.

49 Tschakert, P., and Singha, K., Contaminated identities: mercury and marginalization in Ghana's artisanal mining sector, *Geoforum*, 38/6 (2007): 1304–21.

50 Wesselink, A., Buchanan, K. S., Georgiadou, Y., and Turnhout, E., Technical knowledge, discursive spaces and politics at the science–policy interface, *Environmental Science & Policy*, 30 (2013): 1–9.

51 Spiegel, S., Keane, S., Metcalf, S., and Veiga, M., Implications of the Minamata Convention on Mercury for informal gold mining in sub-Saharan Africa: from global policy debates to grassroots implementation?, *Environment, Development and Sustainability*, 17 (2015): 765–85.

52 Spiegel, S., Keane, S., Metcalf, S., Veiga, M., and Yassi, A., The Minamata Convention on Mercury: time to seek solutions with artisanal mining communities, *Environmental Health Perspectives*, 122/8 (2014): 203–4.

53 Reichardt, C., Heap leaching and the water environment – does low cost recovery come at a high environmental cost?, *International Mine Water Association*, 2008, www.imwa.info/docs/imwa_2008/IMWA2008_008_Reichardt.pdf.

54 Hilson, G., Why is there a large-scale mining 'bias' in sub-Saharan Africa?, *Land Use Policy*, 81 (2019): 852–61.

55 For a study explaining the rise of CSR among mining companies

and differences between their responses, see Dashwood, H., *The Rise of Global Corporate Social Responsibility*. Cambridge: Cambridge University Press, 2013.

56 Cotula, L., *Foreign Investment, Law and Sustainable Development: A Handbook on Agriculture and Extractive Industries*. London: International Institute for Environment and Development, 2014, https://pubs.iied.org/12587IIED/.

57 Ibid.

58 See Humphreys, M., Natural resources, conflict, and conflict resolution – uncovering the mechanisms, *Journal of Conflict Resolution*, 49/4 (2005): 508–37.

59 See Ross, M., What do we know about natural resources and civil war?, *Journal of Peace Research*, 41/3 (2004): 337–56; Le Billon, P., The political ecology of war: natural resources and armed conflicts, *Political Geography*, 20 (2001): 561–84; and Le Billon, Fatal transactions: conflict diamonds and the (anti)terrorist consumer, *Antipode*, 38/4 (2006): 778–801.

60 United Nations, *Extractive Industries and Conflict: Toolkit and Guidance for Preventing and Managing Land and Natural Resources Conflict*. New York: UN Interagency Framework Team for Preventive Action, 2012, www.un.org/en/events/environment-conflictday/pdf/GN_Extractive_Consultation.pdf.

61 See Collier, P., and Hoeffler, A., *Greed and Grievance in Civil War*, Policy Research Working Paper no. 2355. Washington, DC: World Bank, 2001.

62 See Ostby, G., Polarization, horizontal inequalities and violent conflict, *Journal of Peace Research*, 45/2 (2008): 143–62; and Stewart, F., Crisis prevention: tackling horizontal inequalities, *Oxford Development Studies*, 28/3 (2002): 245–62.

63 Silberfein, M., and A. H. Conteh, Boundaries and conflict in the Mano River region of West Africa, *Conflict Management and Peace Science*, 23 (2006): 343–61.

64 United Nations Interregional Crime and Justice Research Institute, *Strengthening the Security and Integrity of the Precious Metals Supply Chain: Technical Report*. Turin: UNCRI, 2016.

65 Callimachi, R., and Klapper, B., Thousands of children work in African gold mines, *New York Times*, 11 August 2008, www.nytimes.com/2008/08/11/world/africa/11iht-mines.4.15181447.html.

66 See Østensen, A. G., and Stridsman, M., *Shadow Value Chains:*

Tracing the Link between Corruption, Illicit Activity and Lootable Natural Resources from West Africa, U4 no. 7. Bergen: Anti-Corruption Resource Centre, 2017.
67 See Martin, A., and Helbig de Balzac, H., *The West Africa El Dorado: Mapping the Illicit Trade of Gold in Côte d'Ivoire, Mali and Burkina Faso*. Ottawa: Partnership Africa Canada, 2017.
68 Østensen and Stridsman, *Shadow Value Chains*, p. 35.
69 Diamonds for Development, *The Current State of Diamond Mining in the Mano River Basin and the Use of Diamonds as a Tool for Peace Building and Development*, Background Paper, Diamonds for Development Sub-regional Conference, Monrovia, Liberia, June 2006, www.international-alert.org/sites/default/files/publications/D4D_Background_report.pdf.
70 Maconachie, R., and Hilson, G., *Mapping Informal Financial Flows in the Artisanal Mining Sector: The Cases of Sierra Leone and Liberia*, Policy Brief no. 39409. London: International Growth Centre, 2019, www.theigc.org/wp-content/uploads/2019/10/Maconachie-and-Hilson-2019-Policy-Brief.pdf.

Chapter 3 An Intractable Industry

1 Bloomfield, M. J., Global production networks and activism: can activists change mining practices by targeting brands?, *New Political Economy*, 22/6 (2017): 727–42.
2 Everett, R., and Gilboy, A., *Impact of the World Bank Group's Social and Environmental Policies on Extractive Companies and Financial Institutions*. Washington, DC: Associates for Global Change, 2003, http://documents.worldbank.org/curated/en/222631468162266718/Associates-for-global-change-impact-of-the-World-Bank-Groups-social-and-environmental-policies-on-extractive-companies-and-financial-institutions-phase-one; Dougherty, M., The global gold mining industry: materiality, rent-seeking, junior firms and Canadian corporate citizenship, *Competition & Change*, 17/4 (2013): 339–54.
3 Bridge, G., Contested terrain: mining and the environment, *Annual Review of Environment and Resources*, 29 (2004): 205–59; Ferguson, J., *Global Shadows: Africa in the Neoliberal World Order*. Durham, NC: Duke University Press, 2006.

4 Bebbington, A., Extractive industries and stunted states: conflict, responsibility and institutional change in the Andes, in R. Raman and R. D. Lipschutz (eds), *Corporate Social Responsibility: Comparative Critiques*. London: Palgrave MacMillan, 2010, pp. 97–115.

5 Dougherty, The global gold mining industry.

6 Ibid.

7 The quotation is attributed to Matthew Zabloski, managing director of Delbrook Capital Advisors Inc., in Vancouver. It first appeared in a Bloomberg news article in 2017. See Owram, K., and Pearson, N. O., In Bre-X country, junior miners crash or post 1,000% gains, *Bloomberg*, 11 October 2017, www.bloomberg.com/news/articles/2017-10-11/in-bre-x-country-junior-miners-can-crash-or-post-1-000-gains.

8 World Bank, Artisanal and small-scale mining, Brief, 21 November 2013, www.worldbank.org/en/topic/extractiveindustries/brief/artisanal-and-small-scale-mining.

9 Hinton, J., *Communities and Small-Scale Mining: An Integrated Review for Development Planning*, 2005, https://asmhub.mn/en/files/view/507.

10 International Labour Organization, *Social and Labour Issues in Small-Scale Mines*, Report TMSSM. Geneva: ILO, 1999; Hinton, *Communities and Small-Scale Mining*.

11 Els, F., Top 10 biggest gold mining companies in the world, 4 July 2019, www.mining.com/featured-article/top-10-biggest-gold-mining-companies/.

12 More information and helpful videos are available on the World Gold Council website at www.gold.org/about-gold/gold-supply/how-gold-is-mined.

13 Persson, T., The world's largest precious metals refineries, 19 August 2016, www.bullionstar.com/blogs/bullionstar/the-worlds-largest-precious-metals-refineries/.

14 Ibid.

15 Pisani, B., How the gold business operates, *CNBC*, 1 September 2011, www.cnbc.com/id/43974868.

16 The Bank of England has a wealth of information available on their website and in their extensive archives. See www.bankofengland.co.uk/.

17 Fortson, D., Fear fills London's fortress of gold, *Sunday Times*,

9 December 2012, www.thetimes.co.uk/article/fear-fills-londons-fortress-of-gold-cbdpzj6ftbc.

18 All figures in this section and the following come from the World Gold Council, available at www.gold.org/goldhub/research/gold-demand-trends/gold-demand-trends-full-year-2018/jewellery.

19 Bloomfield, Global production networks and activism.

20 Solomon, F., and Nicholls, G., *Chain-of-Custody in the Diamond and Gold Jewellery Supply Chain: Issues and Options*, Discussion Paper. Melbourne: Responsible Jewellery Council, 2010, p. 6.

21 Bloomfield, Global production networks and activism.

22 World Gold Council, *Gold Demand Trends: Full Year 2016*. London: World Gold Council, 2017.

23 World Gold Council, *Gold: A Commodity Like No Other*. London: World Gold Council, 2011.

24 World Gold Council, Gold supply, 2019, www.gold.org/about-gold/gold-supply.

25 Olden, P., *Gold and the Jewellery Supply Chain: A Context*. London: Responsible Jewellery Council, 2010, www.responsiblejewellery.com/files/RJC_18_May_Philip_Olden.pdf; Bloomfield, Global production networks and activism.

26 This was discussed in relation to the gold supply chain earlier in the chapter. For further reading on the lack of regard for regulations, see Dougherty, The global gold mining industry; Rees, C., *Report of International Roundtable on Conflict Management and Corporate Culture in the Mining Industry*, Corporate Social Responsibility Initiative Report no. 37. Cambridge, MA: John F. Kennedy School of Government, Harvard University, 2009; Bebbington, A., Extractive industries and stunted states: conflict, responsibility and institutional change in the Andes, in R. Raman and R. D. Lipschutz (eds), *Corporate Social Responsibility: Comparative Critiques*. London: Palgrave Macmillan, 2010, pp. 97–115; Bridge, G., Contested terrain: mining and the environment, *Annual Review of Environment and Resources*, 29 (2004): 205–59.

27 Waldie, P., The rise and fall of Bre-X, *Gold and Mail*, 26 April 2018, www.theglobeandmail.com/report-on-business/the-rise-and-fall-of-bre-x/article1085866/.

28 Brennan, B., David Walsh and the Bre-X Saga, 26 January 2017, http://brianbrennan.ca/david-walsh-and-the-bre-x-saga/.

29 Behar, R., Jungle fever, *Fortune*, 9 June 1997, https://archive.for

tune.com/magazines/fortune/fortune_archive/1997/06/09/227519/
index.htm.

30 Ibid.

31 Ibid.

32 Waldie, The rise and fall of Bre-X.

33 French, C., Bre-X gold scam figure not guilty on all counts,
    Reuters, 31 July 2007, www.reuters.com/article/us-brex-trial-geo
    logist/bre-x-gold-scam-figure-not-guilty-on-all-counts-idUSTOR001
    90620070731?feedType=RSS.

34 Brennan, David Walsh and the Bre-X Saga.

35 Behar, Jungle fever.

36 Ibid.

37 Ibid.

38 Waldie, The rise and fall of Bre-X.

39 Ibid.; Alden, A., The Bre-X gold scandal, history's biggest mining
    fraud, *ThoughtCo*, 3 July 2019, www.thoughtco.com/the-bre-x-
    gold-scandal-1439098.

40 Behar, Jungle fever.

41 Waldie, The rise and fall of Bre-X.

42 Alden, The Bre-X gold scandal.

43 At the time, De Guzman and some other executives were report-
    edly at a Toronto mining conference, hitting up the local strip club,
    'For Your Eyes Only'. Rumour has it that De Guzman proposed to
    a dancer that night but, once rejected, he headed back to Indonesia
    to attend to the site. Other reports have De Guzman at a karaoke
    bar once back, belting out 'My Way' before leaving the following
    day in a helicopter bound for Busang. In any case, he never made
    it. The pilot reported hearing a latch click behind him and, when he
    looked back, his passenger was gone. De Guzman fell 600 feet from
    the helicopter, plunging through the canopy of the Indonesian jun-
    gle. The Indonesian police quickly ruled his death a suicide. When
    his body was finally recovered, days after his fall, his face and limbs
    had been eaten by wild animals, making identification extremely dif-
    ficult. Apparently the Philippines National Bureau of Investigation
    struggled to identify the corpse, while the Indonesian doctor who
    examined the corpse, as well as some investigators in the Philippines,
    expressed some doubt over the cause of death. But, despite the
    rumours circulating, De Guzman's family believes he is dead, and the
    official judgement remains death by suicide. For a gripping retelling

of this sad part of the story, see Wilton, S., The Mystery of Michael De Guzman, *Calgary Herald*, 26 May 2007, https://calgaryherald. com/news/local-news/bre-x-the-real-story-and-scandal-that-inspired-the-movie-gold/wcm/0cdc9284-dfa4-473d-a31e-c212b657149d/.

44 Usborne, D., Bre-X 'world's biggest mining scam', *The Independent*, 6 May 1997, www.independent.co.uk/news/business/bre-x-worlds-biggest-mining-scam-1260057.html.

45 Historical examples of salting are from Groia, J., Badley, J., and Jones, A., *The Aftermath of Bre-X: The Industry's Reaction to the Decision and the Lessons We All Have Learned*, Paper presented at PDAC Conference, Toronto, Canada, 4 March 2008, www.course hero.com/file/48650092/The-Aftermath-of-Bre-X-Mar-4-08pdf/.

46 The Royal Canadian Mounted Police and Indonesian officials launched criminal investigations. At least two class action lawsuits were also announced, one in Canada and one in the US. Walsh never had to face the lawsuit. He died of an apparent stroke at his home in the Bahamas only days after his assets were frozen. Felderhof retreated to his home in the Cayman Islands, a tax haven with no extradition treaty with Canada. In 2007, prospectors continued to search for gold at the Busang site, while, half way around the world, Felderhof was found not guilty of insider trading. The two civil lawsuits were dismissed in 2014. Felderhof died of natural causes on 28 October 2019 in the Philippines, at the age of seventy-nine. He was legally exonerated but struggled to find work in the mining industry after Bre-X. Although most agreed the judge made a reasonable verdict in the Felderhof case, given the evidence available, that doesn't mean there weren't lessons to be learned. For more on the aftermath of the Bre-X scandal, see Alden, The Bre-X gold scandal, history's biggest mining fraud.

47 Heinz, M., Bre-X confirms worst fears: Busang has virtually no gold, *Wall Street Journal*, 5 May 1997, www.wsj.com/articles/SB86279977155130500.

48 Ibid.

49 If it all sounds a bit like a Hollywood film script, that's because it is. A movie based on the story came out in 2017, starring Matthew McConaughey, though for legal reasons the filmmakers changed many details to distance themselves from the true story on which it is clearly based.

50 Wilton, The Mystery of Michael De Guzman.

51 Behar, Jungle fever.
52 Wilton, The Mystery of Michael De Guzman.
53 Ibid.
54 Ibid.
55 *Canada's Public Equities Markets: Your Opportunity*, Toronto Stock Exchange & TSX Venture Exchange, 2014, https://www.tsx.com/ebooks/canadas_public_equities_markets/#10-11.
56 Owram, K., and Pearson, N. O., In Bre-X country, junior miners crash or post 1,000% gains, *Bloomberg*, 11 October 2017, www.bloomberg.com/news/articles/2017-10-11/in-bre-x-country-junior-miners-can-crash-or-post-1-000-gains.
57 Branan, N., Bre-X scandal ends with acquittal, *Geotimes*, October 2007, www.geotimes.org/oct07/article.html?id=nn_bre-x.html.
58 Cited in Schneider, H., A lode of lies: how Bre-X fooled everyone, *Washington Post*, 18 May 1997, www.washingtonpost.com/archive/business/1997/05/18/a-lode-of-lies-how-bre-x-fooled-everyone/e5fd e7ca-e9eb-4c9c-9955-7417213640da/. See also Armstrong, C., *Blue Skies and Boiler Rooms: Buying and Selling Securities in Canada, 1870–1940*. Oxford: Oxford University Press, 1997.

CHAPTER 4 GOLD GOVERNANCE AND GAPS

1 See, Korten, D., *When Corporations Rule the World*. Hartford, CT: Kumarian Press, 1995.
2 The state will usually own the mineral rights even if it doesn't necessarily own the land. But this is not always the case. The details of these arrangements are largely specific to particular jurisdictions, but, whatever the exact details may be in a certain state, the mineral rights owner – public or private – will either sell or lease the rights to develop the deposit to a person or company with the capacity to extract the minerals. As with all elements of the trade, when gold is found, the most powerful actors will flex their muscles to claim their share. The stakes are high, and collecting economic rents from extraction falls within the national interest of the state. In practice, this also means that often state or national government policy will fall afoul of the interests of the local community. If the spoils are not distributed equitably, or impacted communities are not consulted adequately, conflict can and often does arise.

3 See, Otto, J., Andrews, C., Cawood, F., Doggett, M., Guj, P., Stermole, F., Stermole, J., and Tilton, J., *Mining Royalties: A Global Study of Their Impact on Investors, Government, and Civil Society*. Washington, DC: World Bank, 2006; and Bridge, G., Mapping the bonanza: geographies of mining investment in an era of neoliberal reform, *Professional Geographer*, 56/3 (2004): 406–21.

4 Otto et al., *Mining Royalties*.

5 See Campbell, B. (ed.), *Mining in Africa: Regulation and Development*. London: Pluto Press, 2009.

6 See Verisk Maplecroft, Resource nationalism rises in 30 countries: DRC joint highest risk with Venezuela, 21 March 2019, www.maplecroft.com/insights/analysis/resource-nationalism-rises-30-cou ntries/.

7 Kemp, D., and Owen, J., Community relations and mining: core to business but not 'core business', *Resources Policy*, 38/4 (2013): 523–31. See also Newell, P., Citizenship, accountability and community: the limits of the CSR agenda, *International Affairs*, 81 (2005): 541–57; and Hamann, R., Mining companies' role in sustainable development: the 'why' and 'how' of corporate social responsibility from a business perspective, *Development Southern Africa*, 20/2 (2003): 237–54.

8 Moffat, K., and Zhang, A., The paths to social licence to operate: an integrative model explaining community acceptance of mining, *Resources Policy*, 39 (2014): 61–70.

9 For an extended examination into the emergence and development of CSR strategies among major mining companies, including Barrick Gold, see the work of Hevina Dashwood, including *The Rise of Global Corporate Social Responsibility: Mining and the Spread of Global Norms*. Cambridge: Cambridge University Press, 2012; and Sustainable development and industry self-regulation: developments in the global mining sector, *Business & Society*, 43/4 (2013): 551–82.

10 Dupuy, K., Community development requirements in mining laws, *Extractive Industries and Society*, 1/2 (2014): 200–15.

11 EI Sourcebook, *Good Practice Note: Community Development Agreements*, 2011, www.extractiveshub.org/servefile/getFile/id/356.

12 See Gathii, J., and Odumosu-Ayanu, I. T., The turn to contractual responsibility in the global extractive industry, *Business and Human Rights Journal*, 1/1 (2016): 69–94.

13 Nwapi, C., Legal and institutional frameworks for community development agreements in the mining sector in Africa, *Extractive Industries and Society*, 4 (2017): 202–15.

14 Owen, J. R., and Kemp, D., Assets, capitals, and resources: frameworks for corporate community development in mining, *Business & Society*, 51/3 (2012): 382–408.

15 Moody, R., *Rocks and Hard Places: The Globalization of Mining*. London: Zed Books, 2007.

16 Ibid.

17 Industry groups are organisations that look after the interests of their members – companies that operate in a particular market. For example, an industry group may lead the marketing of particular product categories; lobby governments on policy that impacts the industry; liaise with various interest groups on issues of concern; or protect the industry's shared reputation. In short, where there are politics, there are industry groups, and, for gold, there are many such groups.

18 Matejova, M., Parker, S., and Dauvergne, P., The politics of repressing environmentalists as agents of foreign influence, *Australian Journal of International Affairs*, 72/2 (2018): 145–62.

19 See, for example, Bartley, T., and Child, C., Shaming the corporation: the social production of targets and the anti-sweatshop movement, *American Sociological Review*, 79/4 (2014): 653–79; Dauvergne, P., Is the power of brand-focused activism rising? The case of tropical deforestation, *Journal of Environment and Development*, 26/2 (2017): 135–55; Bloomfield, M. J., Shame campaigns and environmental justice: corporate shaming as activist strategy, *Environmental Politics*, 23/2 (2014): 263–81; Baron, D., and Diermeier, D., Strategic activism and non-market strategy, *Journal of Economics and Management Strategy*, 16/3 (2007): 599–634.

20 Keck, M. E., and Sikkink, K., *Activists beyond Borders: Advocacy Networks in International Politics*. Ithaca, NY: Cornell University Press, 1998; Khagram, S., Riker, J. V., and Sikkink, K., *Restructuring World Politics: Transnational Social Movements, Networks, and Norms*. Minneapolis: University of Minnesota Press, 2002.

21 Schurman, R., Fighting 'Frankenfoods': industry opportunity structures and the efficacy of the anti-biotech movement in Western

Europe, *Social Problems*, 51/2 (2004): 243–68; Klein, N., *No Logo: Taking Aim at the Brand Bullies*. New York: Picador, 1999; Baron and Diermeier, Strategic activism and non-market strategy.

22 For a full account of the No Dirty Campaign, the industry response, and the implications for environmental politics and corporate accountability, see Bloomfield, M. J., *Dirty Gold: How Activism Transformed the Jewelry Industry*. Cambridge, MA: MIT Press, 2017.

23 Since the 1990s, these campaigns have become increasingly familiar to both brands and consumers. One of the best-known examples is the campaign to eradicate 'sweatshops' – factories with poor working conditions where workers toil long hours for low wages. The campaign targeted Nike and other branded apparel companies, even though these big brands didn't own or operate the factories directly. It was instead an attempt to hold these large buyers responsible for the conditions in the factories from which they were buying their garments and footwear and to compel them to put pressure on their suppliers to change their labour practices. A campaign launched by the NGO Rainforest Action Network relied on a similar direct targeting strategy. This targeted the large DIY retailers Home Depot, B&Q and comparable companies in an attempt to leverage their brand and market share to change the practices of the forestry companies that supplied them. For more on campaigns in the apparel sector, see Gereffi, G., Garcia-Johnson, R., and Sasser, E., The NGO–industrial complex, *Foreign Policy*, 125/4 (2001): 56–65; Bartley, T., Certifying forests and factories: states, social movements, and the rise of private regulation in the apparel and forest products fields, *Politics & Society*, 31/3 (2003): 433–64. For more on campaigns in the forestry sector, see Sasser, E., Gaining leverage: NGO influence on certification institutions in the forest products sector, in L. Teeter, B. Cashore and D. Zhang (eds), *Forest Policy for Private Forestry: Global and Regional Challenges*. Wallingford: CABI, 2003, pp. 229–44; Sasser, E., Prakash, A., Cashore, B., and Auld, G., Direct targeting as an NGO political strategy: examining private authority regimes in the forestry sector, *Business and Politics*, 8/3 (2006): 1–32; Bartley, Certifying forests and factories.

24 To learn more about diamonds and the campaign against 'conflict' or 'blood' diamonds, including critiques of the Kimberly Process

Certification Scheme, see Smillie, I., *Diamonds*. Cambridge: Polity, 2014.

25 To understand why there was variation in corporate responses, see Bloomfield, *Dirty Gold*.

26 See the No Dirty Gold campaign website for an up-to-date list: https://earthworks.org/campaigns/no-dirty-gold/retailers/the_gold_star_list/#.Ukmtk7zj8aQ.

27 This quotation is an excerpt from an interview between Michael Rae, the former RJC CEO, and Greg Valerio, a jeweller and activist. The full interview transcript was reproduced on a prominent industry blog by another jeweller-activist, Marc Choyt: Greg Valerio interviews Michael Rae, CEO of the Responsible Jewellery Council, 29 June 2009, https://fairjewelry.org/greg-valerio-interviews-michael-rae-ceo-of-the-responsible-jewellery-council/.

28 For more on the increasingly transnational governance landscape of gold, see Auld, G., Betsill, M., and VanDeveer, S. D., Transnational governance for mining and the mineral lifecycle, *Annual Review of Environment and Resources*, 43 (2018): 425–53; Heidingsfelder, J., Private sustainability governance in the making – a case study analysis of the fragmentation of sustainability governance for the gold sector, *Resources Policy*, 63 (2019): 101462.

29 Fairtrade believes that the potential for the greatest impact of certification lies with artisanal miners. There are other organisations that support improvements in medium- and large-scale mining, such as the Responsible Jewellery Council. For more on Fairtrade gold and, in particular, stakeholder responses to it, see Sippl, K. L., *Southern Responses to Fair Trade Gold: Cooperation, Competition, Supplementation*, Harvard Business School Working Paper 19-055, 2019, www.hbs.edu/faculty/Publication%20Files/19-055_5c205f81-6d63-4da0-8210-365ab43d9de5.pdf.

30 See Anderson, F., Good as Fairtrade gold, *HuffPost*, 29 September 2016, www.huffingtonpost.co.uk/fi-anderson/good-as-fairtrade-gold_b_12246420.html?guccounter=1&guce_referrer=aHR0cHM6Ly93d3cuZ29vZ2xlLmNvbS8&guce_referrer_sig=AQAAAIAUfbYZc8E4LnHH0Z6sd9GiaxVFXFb0DaEUv4RZLtJFfyl0-JQI4CxPTO4A-RODsQEhAhi7sz_PGcMA8a8OW2mPr5VSsJUWHremsi5DVJ4HZvI9I8ITSNTSYpEmO74k4satpwGix6kqSai_eDVqNSLi0iYBXfbCpVzsclfxpj7t.

31 Kinniburgh, C., Beyond 'conflict minerals': the Congo's resource

curse lives on, *Dissent*, 61/2 (2014), www.dissentmagazine.org/arti
cle/beyond-conflict-minerals-the-congos-resource-curse-lives-on.

32 Wemer, D. A., 'Conflict gold' fueling war in the Democratic Republic of the Congo, *New Atlanticist*, 26 October 2018, www.atlanticcouncil.org/blogs/new-atlanticist/conflict-gold-fueling-war-in-the-democratic-republic-of-the-congo/.

33 Cited ibid., p. 2.

34 Valerio, G., Conflict free gold? A quick look at the World Gold Council's draft standard consultation document on conflict free chain of custody for large-scale mined gold, 2011, https://gregvalerio.com/mining/small-scale-mining/conflict-free-gold/.

35 See SARW/OSISA, *The High Cost of Congolese Gold: Poverty, Abuse and the Collapse of Family and Community Structures*, 2013, www.extractiveshub.org/servefile/getFile/id/1000, p. 16.

36 Wemer, 'Conflict gold' fueling war in the Democratic Republic of the Congo.

37 Senese, K., Conflict gold from Africa may be in U.S. markets, passing through major companies, *Spend Matters*, 6 November 2018, https://spendmatters.com/2018/11/06/study-conflict-gold-from-africa-may-be-in-u-s-markets-passing-through-major-companies/.

38 Dranginis, H., *Going for Gold: Engaging the Jewelry Industry in Responsible Gold Sourcing in Africa's Great Lakes Region*, Enough Project, November 2014, https://enoughproject.org/files/publications/GoingForGold-EnoughProject-Nov2014.pdf.

39 Bafilemba, F., and Lezhnev, S., *Congo's Conflict Gold Rush: Bringing Gold into the Legal Trade in the Democratic Republic of the Congo*, Enough Project, April 2015, https://enoughproject.org/files/April%2029%202015%20Congo%20Conflict%20Gold%20Rush%20reduced.pdf.

40 O'Gorman, E., *Conflict and Development*. London: Zed Books, 2011.

41 Geenen, S., A dangerous bet: the challenges of formalizing artisanal mining in the Democratic Republic of Congo, *Resources Policy*, 37/3 (2012): 322–30.

42 See ibid., pp. 327–8.

43 See Cuvelier, J., Van Bockstael, S., Vlassenroot, K., and Iguma, C., *Analyzing the Impact of the Dodd–Frank Act on Congolese Livelihoods*. New York: Social Science Research Council, Conflict Prevention and Peace Forum, 2014, https://s3.amazonaws.com/

ssrc-cdn1/crmuploads/new_publication_3/analyzing-the-impact-of-the-dodd-frank-act-on-congolese-livelihoods.pdf, p. 10.

44 Seay, L. E., *What's Wrong with Dodd–Frank 1502? Conflict Minerals, Civilian Livelihoods, and the Unintended Consequences of Western Advocacy*, Working Paper 284, Centre for Global Development, 2012, www.cgdev.org/sites/default/files/1425843_file_Seay_Dodd_Frank_FINAL.pdf.

45 Filitz, J., The Dodd–Frank repeal: what it means for conflict minerals, 2017, www.mining.com/web/dodd-frank-repeal-means-conflict-minerals/.

46 Ille, E., Complications in the classification of conflict areas and conflicts actors for the identification of 'conflict gold' from Sudan, *Extractive Industries and Society*, 3/1 (2016): 193–203.

47 Østensen, A. G., and Stridsman, M., *Shadow Value Chains: Tracing the Link between Corruption, Illicit Activity and Lootable Natural Resources from West Africa*, U4 no. 7. Bergen: Anti-Corruption Resource Centre, 2017.

48 Seay, *What's Wrong with Dodd–Frank 1502?*

49 For example, Kamath, R., Crypto-governance blockchain governance for Sustainable Development Goals 16 and 17, *Journal of Poverty Alleviation & International Development*, 9/2 (2018): 111–28; Galvez, J. F., Mejuto, J. C., and Simal-Gandara, J., Future challenges on the use of blockchain for food traceability analysis, *Trends in Analytical Chemistry*, 107 (2018): 222–32; Agrawal, T. K., Sharma, A., and Kumar, V., Blockchain-based secured traceability system for textile and clothing supply chain, in S. Thomassey and X. Zeng (eds), *Artificial Intelligence for Fashion Industry in the Big Data Era*. Singapore: Springer, 2018, pp. 197–208.

50 Visser, C., and Hanich, Q., How blockchain is strengthening tuna traceability to combat illegal fishing, *The Conversation*, 21 January 2018, https://theconversation.com/how-blockchain-is-strengthening-tuna-traceability-to-combat-illegal-fishing-89965.

51 Calvão, F., and Gronwald, V., *Blockchain in the Mining Industry: Implications for Sustainable Development in Africa*, Policy Insights no. 74. Johannesburg: South African Institute of International Affairs, 2019, www.africaportal.org/documents/19479/Policy_Insights_74.pdf.

52 Hobson, P., London gold association plans to approve blockchain

trackers, *Reuters*, 19 October 2018, www.reuters.com/article/gold-blockchain-lbma/london-gold-association-plans-to-approve-block chain-trackers-idUSL8N1WX5N4.

53 Wieczner, J., Gold-backed cryptocurrency is almost here, *Fortune*, 11 March 2019, https://fortune.com/2019/03/11/gold-cryptocur rency-stocks-blockchain/.

54 The future of gold rests with blockchain, says Sprott CEO, *Kitco News*, 7 May 2019, www.kitco.com/news/2019-05-07/The-Future-Of-Gold-Rests-With-Blockchain-Says-Sprott-CEO.html.

55 For more information, see Shadbolt, P., How blockchain is changing gold markets, 11 April 2017, www.royalmint.com/articles/invest/how-blockchain-is-changing-gold-markets/. See also Faden, M., Britain's Royal Mint trades gold in blockchain transactions, *American Express*, 2019, www.americanexpress.com/us/foreign-exchange/articles/blockchain-transactions-digital-trade-gold/.

56 Trustchain is a brand new initiative developed by IBM, in collaboration with various industry actors, including, for example, Rio Tinto.

57 Holmes, F., Blockchain will completely revolutionize how we mine gold and precious metals, 22 May 2018, www.mining.com/web/blockchain-will-completely-revolutionize-mine-gold-precious-met als/.

58 Brugger, F., Blockchain is great, but it can't solve everything – take conflict minerals, *African Arguments*, 23 April 2019, https://african arguments.org/2019/04/23/blockchain-is-great-but-it-cant-solve-eve rything-take-conflict-minerals/.

59 Calvão and Gronwald, *Blockchain in the Mining Industry*.

60 Morrison, S., Fairtrade: is it really fair? *The Independent*, 6 May 2012, www.independent.co.uk/news/world/politics/fairtrade-is-it-really-fair-7717624.html

61 Sylla, N. S., Fairtrade is an unjust movement that serves the rich, *The Guardian*, 5 September 2014, www.theguardian.com/global-development/2014/sep/05/fairtrade-unjust-movement-serves-rich.

62 WWF, *A Precious Transition: Demanding More Transparency and Responsibility in the Watch and Jewellery Sector: Environmental Rating and Industry Report 2018*, www.wwf.ch/sites/default/files/doc-2018-12/2018_12_07_WWF%20Watch%20and%20Jewellery%20Report%202018_final_e_0.pdf.

63 Neate, R., Rio Tinto accused of environmental and human rights

breaches, *The Guardian*, 18 April 2013, www.theguardian.com/business/2013/apr/18/rio-tinto-environmental-human-rights-breaches.

64 WWF, *A Precious Transition*.

CHAPTER 5 RISING POWERS IN SUPPLY AND DEMAND

1 World Gold Council, Investing in gold: going mainstream, 2019, www.gold.org/what-we-do/investing-gold/why-invest-gold/mainstream-investing-in-gold.
2 Counter-cyclical simply means that the price tends to rise when the economy is weakening and to fall when the economy gets stronger.
3 World Gold Council, Investing in gold.
4 Ibid.
5 Clapp, J., Financialization, distance and global food politics, *Journal of Peasant Studies*, 41/5 (2014): 797–814.
6 Ibid.; see also Bloomfield, M. J., Global production networks and activism: can activists change mining practices by targeting brands?, *New Political Economy*, 22/6 (2017): 727–42.
7 Olden, P., *Gold and the Jewellery Supply Chain: A Context*. London: Responsible Jewellery Council, 2010, www.responsiblejewellery.com/files/RJC_18_May_Philip_Olden.pdf; Hewitt, A., Keel, T., Tauber, M., and Le-Fiedler, T., *The Ups and Downs of Gold Recycling: Understanding Market Drivers and Industry Challenges* (London: World Gold Council and Boston Consulting Group, 2015), www.gxgold.com.cn/uploads/2017/06/100103511216.pdf; and Bloomfield, Global production networks and activism.
8 World Gold Council, How to buy gold, 2019, www.gold.org/what-we-do/gold-investment/how-buy-gold.
9 Ibid.
10 World Gold Council, Major global trading hubs, 2019, www.gold.org/what-we-do/gold-market-structure/global-gold-market.
11 Ibid.
12 London Bullion Market Association, www.lbma.org.uk; Bloomfield, Global production networks and activism.
13 Ennis, T. W., Exchanges ready for gold trading, *New York Times*, 8 February 1972, www.nytimes.com/1972/02/08/archives/exchanges-ready-for-gold-trading-futures-in-metal-planned-for-new.html.

14 We have already discussed Turkey's gold purchases in chapter 1. Kazakhstan's large purchases are explained by a surge in domestic gold production coupled with a policy of buying gold with its significant oil and gas export earnings.

15 GFMS, *Gold Survey 2019*. London: Thomas Reuters GFMS, 2019; see also Sanderson, H., China doubles down on gold in shift away from dollar, *Financial Times*, 12 March 2019, www.ft.com/content/1cb92e5a-43e6-11e9-b168-96a37d002cd3.

16 Comparisons vary, but see for example the February 2017 report by PwC, *The World in 2050*, www.pwc.com/gx/en/issues/economy/the-world-in-2050.html.

17 As quoted in van Vuuren, R. J., BRICS gold: a new model for multilateral cooperation, *Mining Review Africa*, 27 July 2018, www.miningreview.com/top-stories/brics-gold-new-model-multilateral-co operation/.

18 Ibid.

19 As cited in Manly, R., Russia, China and BRICS: a new gold trading network, *Bullion Star*, 2 December 2017, www.bullionstar.com/blogs/ronan-manly/russia-china-new-gold-trading-network/;   also reported by the Russian news agency TASS, https://tass.com/econ omy/977276.

20 Manly, Russia, China and BRICS.

21 Statistics from World Gold Council's *Goldhub*, 2019, www.gold.org/goldhub/data/historical-mine-production.

22 Markets Insider, 2020, https://markets.businessinsider.com/comm odities/news/gold-countries-that-hold-largest-reserves-2019-4-1028 128947#10-india1.

23 Statista, Gold reserves of largest gold holding countries worldwide, December   2019,   www.statista.com/statistics/267998/countries-with-the-largest-gold-reserves/.

24 Ibid.

25 GFMS, *Gold Survey 2019*.

26 Bloomfield, M. J., *Dirty Gold: How Activism Transformed the Jewelry Industry*. Cambridge, MA: MIT Press, 2017; Bloomfield, Global production networks and activism; World Gold Council, *Gold Demand Trends: Full Year 2014*, 2015, www.agloc.org/pdf/GDT_Q4_2014.pdf.

27 Bloomfield, *Dirty Gold*, and Global production networks and activism; World Gold Council. Gold demand trends: first quarter

2012, www.perthmintbullion.com/blog/blog/12-05-18/World_Gold _Council_Gold_Demand_Trends_First_Quarter_2012.aspx; Statista, Consumer gold demand in major consuming countries 2015, www. statista.com/statistics/299638/gold-consumer-demand-by-top-consu ming-country/.

28 See company website for more details: www.chinagoldintl.com/cor porate/overview/.

29 The Economist, The price of gold, *The Economist*, 6 April 2013, www.economist.com/china/2013/04/06/the-price-of-gold.

30 See, for example, Cheng, A. L. H., The growing and evolving gold retail investment market in China, *Alchemist*, no. 68 (a publication of the LBMA), 2012, www.lbma.org.uk/assets/blog/alchemist_arti cles/Alch68Cheng.pdf. Note that Cheng is the managing director, Far East, World Gold Council.

31 World Gold Council, *China's Gold Market: Progress and Prospects*. London: World Gold Council, 2014.

32 World Gold Council, *India's Gold Market: Evolution and Innovation*. London: World Gold Council, 2017.

33 Ablett, J., Baijal, A., Beinhocker, E., Bose, A., Farrell, D., Gersch, U., Greenberg, E., Gupta, S., and Gupta S., *The 'Bird of Gold': The Rise of India's Consumer Market*. London: McKinsey & Co., 2007, www.mckinsey.com/~/media/mckinsey/featured%20insights/ Asia%20Pacific/The%20bird%20of%20gold/MGI_Rise_of_Indian _Consumer_Market_full_report.ashx.

34 See, for example, World Gold Council, *India's Gold Market*; see also Ablett et al., *The 'Bird of Gold'*.

35 Afonso, S., and Karve, A., The battle for India's $45 billion gold industry has begun, *Bloomberg*, 31 August 2017, www.bloom bergquint.com/business/the-battle-for-india-s-45-billion-gold-indus try-has-begun.

36 Ibid.

37 As quoted ibid.

38 Numbers come from the company website: www.rajeshindia.com/.

39 Bhayani, R., Thanks to refining industry, unrefined gold import surges to a new high, *Business Standard India*, 2 November 2018, www.business-standard.com/article/markets/india-meets-half-of-do mestic-gold-demand-from-importing-unrefined-gold-11811010078 9_1.html.

40 World Gold Council, *India's Gold Market*.

41 Bloomfield, *Dirty Gold*.

42 Bloomfield, Global production networks and activism.

43 See, for example, Naim, M., Rogue aid, *Foreign Policy*, 15 October 2009, https://foreignpolicy.com/2009/10/15/rogue-aid/; but see also Dreher, A., and Fuchs, A., Rogue aid? An empirical analysis of China's aid allocation, *Canadian Journal of Economics/Revue canadienne d'économique*, 48/3 (2015): 988–1023.

44 Cai, Z., and Aguilar, F. X., Consumer stated purchasing preferences and corporate social responsibility in the wood products industry: a conjoint analysis in the U.S. and China, *Ecological Economics*, 95 (2013): 118–27; Iweala, S., and Sun, S., The many aspects of sustainability governance: unpacking consumers' support for tea standards in China and the UK, Paper presented at the 2019 Earth System Conference, Oaxaca, Mexico, 2019; Fesenfeld, L. P., Wicki, M., Sun, Y., and Bernauer, T., Policy packaging can make food system transformation feasible, *Nature Food*, 1/3 (2020): 173–82.

45 World Gold Council representative, personal communication, 18 July 2012.

46 Statistics from World Gold Council, *Gold Demand Trends: Full Year 2016*. London: World Gold Council, 2017.

47 For an extended discussion of the opportunities and limits of the No Dirty Gold campaign, see Bloomfield, Global production networks and activism.

CHAPTER 6 CONCLUSION

1 World Gold Council, *Gold: A Commodity Like No Other*. London: World Gold Council, 2011.

2 Bridge, G., and LeBillon, P., *Oil*. Cambridge: Polity, 2017.

3 Nest, M., *Coltan*. Cambridge: Polity, 2011; Smillie, I., *Diamonds*. Cambridge: Polity, 2014; Laudati, A., Beyond minerals: broadening 'economies of violence' in eastern Democratic Republic of Congo, *Review of African Political Economy*, 40/135 (2013): 32–50.

4 Richardson, B., *Sugar*. Cambridge: Polity, 2015; Dauvergne, P., and Lister, J., *Timber*. Cambridge: Polity, 2011.

5 Clapp, J., *Food*. Cambridge: Polity, 2016; Fridell, G., *Coffee*. Cambridge: Polity, 2014.

6 For example, see Banchirigah, S. M., and Hilson, G., De-agrarianization, *re*-agrarianization and local economic development: re-orientating livelihoods in African artisanal mining communities, *Policy Sciences*, 43 (2010): 157–80; Hirons, M., Shifting sand, shifting livelihoods? Reflections on a coastal gold rush in Ghana, *Resources Policy*, 40/1 (2013): 83–9; Hilson, G., Small-scale mining, poverty and economic development in sub-Saharan Africa: an overview, *Resources Policy*, 34/1–2 (2009): 1–5; Maconachie, R., and Binns, T., 'Farming miners' or 'mining farmers'? Diamond mining and rural development in post-conflict Sierra Leone, *Journal of Rural Studies*, 23/3 (2007): 367–80.

7 Maconachie and Binns, 'Farming miners' or 'mining farmers'?

8 Maconachie, R., Re-agrarianising livelihoods in post-conflict Sierra Leone? Mineral wealth and rural change in artisanal and small-scale mining communities, *Journal of International Development*, 23/8 (2011): 1054–67.

9 For example, see Shepherd, D. A., and Patzelt, H., The new field of sustainable entrepreneurship: studying entrepreneurial action linking 'What is to be sustained' with 'What is to be developed', *Entrepreneurship Theory and Practice*, 25/1 (2011): 137–63.

10 See Maconachie, R., and G. Hilson, Artisanal gold mining: a new frontier in post-conflict Sierra Leone?, *Journal of Development Studies*, 47/4 (2011): 595–616.

11 For example, see Fisher, E., Occupying the margins: labour integration and social exclusion in artisanal mining in Tanzania, *Development and Change*, 38/4 (2007): 735–60; Bashwira, M. R., Cuvelier, J., Hilhorst, D., and van der Haar, G., Not only a man's world: women's involvement in artisanal mining in eastern DRC, *Resources Policy*, 40 (2014): 109–16; Hilson, G., Hilson, A., Siwale, A., and Maconachie, R., Female faces in informal 'spaces': women and artisanal and small-scale mining in sub-Saharan Africa, *Africa Journal of Management*, 4/3 (2018): 306–46; and Buss, D., Rutherford, B., Stewart, J., Côté, G. A., Sebina-Zziwa, A., Kibombo, R., Hinton, J., and Lebert, J., Gender and artisanal and small-scale mining: implications for formalization, *Extractive Industries and Society*, 6/4 (2019): 1101–12.

Selected Readings

Readers interested in the Serra Pelada mines, the real life moonscape located on Genesio Ferreira da Silva's land, really need to check out the haunting photos by the Brazilian photographer Sebastião Salgado. They are easily searchable on the internet. To place it in wider context, see also Helmut Waszkis, *Mining in the Americas: Stories and History* (Cambridge: Woodhead, 1993). For a more critical, political ecology analysis, readers should see Anthony Bebbington and Jeffrey Bury (eds), *Subterranean Struggles: New Dynamics of Mining, Oil, and Gas in Latin America* (Austin: University of Texas Press, 2013).

The World Gold Council provides a wealth of information on all aspects of the gold industry in terms of statistics and market trends, not to mention their 'Conflict-Free Gold Standard'. Go to their website at www.gold.org and browse or search their reports there for supply chain information. They have documents we have referenced throughout the book, on gold supply and demand, financial markets, and industry actors and standards.

For an annual look at gold markets around the world, the annual GFMS reports are invaluable. See, for example, *Gold Survey 2019* (London: Thomas Reuters GFMS Ltd). Access to these consultancy reports can cost quite a bit of money, but often libraries will have permission. For example, the British Library in London has subscriptions to many databases and market analyses in their Business and IP Centre.

For a good overall read on the history of gold, try Peter L. Bernstein, *The Power of Gold: The History of an Obsession* (Chichester: Wiley, 2004).

On ASM mining and development opportunities, see Gavin Hilson and Roy Maconachie, Artisanal and small-scale mining and the Sustainable Development Goals: opportunities and new directions for sub Saharan Africa, *Geoforum*, 111 (2020): 125–41; and Roy Maconachie and Tony Binns (2007) 'Farming miners' or 'mining farmers'? Diamond mining and rural development in post-conflict Sierra Leone, *Journal of Rural Studies*, 23(3) (2007): 367–80. For a recent analysis of the impacts of large-scale mining on ASM communities in the DRC, see Ben Radley, A distributional analysis of artisanal and industrial wage levels and expenditure in the Congolese mining sector, *Journal of Development Studies*, 2020, https://doi.org/10.1080 /00220388.2020.1725484.

For those interested in small-scale diamond mining, see Roy Maconachie and Simon Wharf's film *Voices from the Mine: Artisanal Diamonds and Resource Governance in Sierra Leone* (2018), which can be viewed for free at, https://vimeo. com/268739048/89901d8c30.

On extractive industries and communities, see June Nash, *We Eat the Mines and the Mines Eat Us: Dependency and Exploitation in Bolivian Tin Mines* (New York: Columbia University Press, 1993). Although not specifically about gold mining, this classic read is a powerful anthropological study of a Bolivian tin mining town, which explores the influence of modern industrialization on the traditional culture of Quechua- and Aymara-speaking Indians.

For a classic piece of scholarship on the negative development impacts of mining in Africa, see Greg Lanning and Marti Mueller's, *Africa Undermined: Mining Companies and the Underdevelopment of Africa* (Harmondsworth: Penguin, 1979).

On conflict diamonds, see Ian Smillie's book in this series: *Diamonds* (Cambridge: Polity, 2014); and his earlier work *Blood on the Stone: Greed, Corruption and War in the Global Diamond Trade* (London: Anthem Press, 2010).

For a classic piece on social movements and resistance, see Anthony Bebbington, Denise Humphreys Bebbington, Jeffrey Bury, Jeannet Lingan, Juan Pablo Muñoz and Martin Scurrah (2008) Mining and social movements: struggles over livelihood and rural territorial development in the Andes, *World Development*, 36(12) (2008): 2888–905.

For a great piece on mining and development, see Anthony Bebbington, Leonith Hinojosa, Denise Humphreys Bebbington, Maria Luisa Burneo and Ximena Warnaars, Contention and ambiguity: mining and the possibilities of development, *Development and Change*, 39 (2008): 887–914.

For a review article that critically surveys an extensive literature on mining, development and environment, see Gavin Bridge (2004) Contested terrain: mining and the environment, *Annual Review of Environment and Resources*, 29 (2004): 205–59.

On mining 'enclaves' and a sharp, critical analysis of the mining sector, read James Ferguson, *Global Shadows: Africa in the Neoliberal World Order* (Durham, NC: Duke University Press, 2006).

On large-scale mining and the SDGs, see *Mapping Mining to the Sustainable Development Goals: A Preliminary Atlas* (New York: United Nations Development Programme, 2016). But also read up on the latest report by the independent Responsible Mining Foundation, which is much more critical and accuses mining companies of 'SDG-washing' by focusing only on the positives. This can be found on the very informative Responsible Mining Index website: https://2020.responsibleminingindex.org/en.

Those wanting to read up on the globalisation of the mining sector could check out Roger Moody, *Rocks and Hard Places: The Globalization of Mining* (London: Zed Books, 2007). A related and fantastic article is by Gavin Bridge: Mapping the bonanza: geographies of mining investment in an era of neoliberal reform, *Professional Geographer*, 56 (2004): 406–21.

On governing the mining industry, read this multi-case analysis of the history and political economy of governing extractive industries in Latin America and Africa: Anthony Bebbington, Abdul-Gafaru Abdulai, Denise Humphreys Bebbington, Marja Hinfelaar, and Cynthia A. Sanborn, *Governing Extractive Industries: Politics, Histories, Ideas* (Oxford: Oxford University Press, 2018).

For an informative piece on mining and climate change, see Scott D. Odell, Anthony Bebbington, and Karen E. Frey (2018) Mining and climate change: a review and framework for analysis, *Extractive Industries and Society*, 5 (2018): 201–14.

Readers looking for additional analyses and mapping of the fragmented and transnational governance landscape of gold mining can consult Graeme Auld, Michele Betsill and Stacy D. VanDeveer, Transnational governance for mining and the mineral lifecycle, *Annual Review of Environment and Resources*, 43(2018): 425–53; and Jens Heidingsfelder, Private sustainability governance in the making – a case study analysis of the fragmentation of sustainability governance for the gold sector, *Resources Policy*, 63 (2019): 101462.

On the rise of CSR among gold mining companies, read Hevina S. Dashwood, *The Rise of Global Corporate Social Responsibility: Mining and the Spread of Global Norms* (Cambridge: Cambridge University Press, 2012).

For further work on the activist direct targeting campaigns, see Naomi Klein's *No Logo: Taking Aim at the Brand Bullies* (New York: Picador, 1999). There are plenty of journal articles as well, of course. See Tim Bartley and Curtis Child, Shaming the corporation: the social production of targets and the anti-sweatshop movement, *American Sociological Review*, 79 (2014): 653–79; Peter Dauvergne, Is the power of brand-focused activism rising? The case of tropical deforestation, *Journal of Environment & Development*, 26 (2017): 135–55; and Michael John Bloomfield, Shame campaigns and environmental justice: corporate shaming as activist strategy, *Environmental Politics*, 23 (2014): 263–81.

On transnational activist networks, see Margaret E. Keck and Kathryn Sikkink, *Activists beyond Borders: Advocacy Networks in International Politics* (Ithaca, NY: Cornell University Press, 1998); Sanjeev Khagram, James V. Riker and Kathryn Sikkink, *Restructuring World Politics: Transnational Social Movements, Networks, and Norms* (Minneapolis: University of Minnesota Press, 2002). For a critical lens on some forms of transnational activism, see Peter Dauvergne and Genevieve LeBaron, *Protest Inc.: The Corporatization of Activism* (Cambridge: Polity, 2014).

On corporate responses to activism, see Michael John Bloomfield, *Dirty Gold: How Activism Transformed the Jewelry Industry* (Cambridge, MA: MIT Press, 2017). This will also give readers a full account of the No Dirty Campaign, the industry response, and the implications for environmental politics and corporate accountability. In terms of scholarly articles, some great ones are Rachel Schurman, Fighting 'Frankenfoods': industry opportunity structures and the efficacy of the anti-biotech movement in Western Europe, *Social Problems*, 51 (2004): 243–68; David P. Baron and Daniel Diermeier, Strategic activism and non-market strategy, *Journal of Economics & Management Strategy*, 16 (2007): 599–634.

To read more on the financialisation of commodities and its impact on sustainability, see works by Jennifer Clapp, whose writing is mostly in relation to food supply chains, but very relevant. See, for example, her book in this series: *Food* (3rd edn, Cambridge: Polity, 2020). For the journal article we referenced in the chapter on financialisation, see Financialization, distance and global food politics, *Journal of Peasant Studies*, 41 (2014): 797–814.

As gender has increasingly become recognised as a key area of focus in development studies, a number of important journal articles have recently focused on gender and artisanal mining. For example, see Marie-Bashwira, Jeroen Cuvelier, Dorothea Hilhorst and Gemma van der Haar, Not only a man's world: women's involvement in artisanal mining in eastern DRC, *Resources Policy*, 40 (2014): 109–16; Chris Huggins, Doris Buss and Blair Rutherford, A 'cartography of concern': place-making practices and gender in the artisanal mining sector in Africa, *Geoforum*, 83 (2017): 142–52; or Gavin Hilson, Abigail Hilson, Agatha Siwale and Roy Maconachie (2018) Female faces in informal 'spaces': women and artisanal and small-scale mining in sub-Saharan Africa, *Africa Journal of Management*, 4 (2018): 306–46.

Also see chapter 11, 'Women and artisanal mining: gender roles and the road ahead', by Jennifer Hinton, Marcello Viega and Christian Bienhoff, in *The Socio-Economic Impacts of Artisanal and Small-Scale Mining in Developing Countries*, ed. G. Hilson (Lisse: A. A. Balkema, 2003).

In the Open Knowledge Repository of the World Bank, readers may also like to explore *Gender Dimensions of Artisanal and Small-Scale Mining: A Rapid Assessment Toolkit* (2012), available at https://openknowledge.worldbank.org/handle/10986/2731.

Index

accountability 31, 32, 33, 114,
    116
activists 8, 10, 38, 138–9, 140, 142,
    150–1
  corporate direct targeting 86
  Earthworks 86–8
  Enough Project 96–7, 101
  Fairtrade Gold movement 94–6
  financialisation and 143
  global activists 84–5
  No Dirty Gold campaign 86–92
  Responsible Business Alliance (RBA)
    97–8
  shame campaigns 86
  traceability 96–100
Africa
  Chinese mining operations 25, 26
  colonial expansion 18
  conflict in West Africa 38, 41–3
  sub-Saharan 27–8, 80, 97
  see also Ghana; Mali
the Amazon
  Brazil 126–7
  Colombia 4–5
  gold rushes 1–2, 3–4, 44, 127
  lootable resources 41–2
  NTR Metals and 4, 106
  Peru 110
  Serra Pelada mine 1–2
Amster, Hillary 98
Antarctica 52
Argentina, Veladero mine 27
Argor-Heraeus SA 58, 110
Armstrong, Christopher 75

artisanal small-scale gold mining
    (ASGM) 12, 23, 151
  blockchain and 108
  child labour 23, 96
  China and 27–8
  conflict and 40–2
  as driver of development 146–9
  ecological impacts 34–6
  Fairtrade and 94–6
  gendered aspects 149
  gold production per annum 23
  lax regulation 34, 40, 41
  nature of 23, 51–2, 56
  numbers employed in 23, 51, 52
  sustainable development goals 146–9
  women in 23, 96, 148–9
Asian Infrastructure Development Bank
    123
Atilla, Mehmet Hakan 154n8
Australia
  Chinese mining operations 27, 130–1
  gold production 125
  gold reserves 126
  Victoria Gold Rush (1851) 19

Bank of England 60
bank vaults 60
Barclays 60–1
Barrick Gold 27, 70, 71, 130
Bebbington, Tony 50
Behar, Richard 69, 70
Bernstein, Peter 13
BHP Billiton 51
Bingham Canyon Mine, Utah 56

Binns, Tony 147
bitcoin 106, 107
blockchain 105–8
blood diamonds 4, 87
Botchwey, Gabriel 28
Brazil
    Amazon Gold Rush 126–7
    gold reserves 127
    see also BRICS
Bretton Woods 21
Bre-X Minerals 66–76
BRICS 11, 119–23, 138
    divergence among members 121–2
    GDP 119–20
    gold and 123–8
    gradualism 122
    Kluchevskoye Gold Mining Project
        118–19, 123–4
    single gold trading system 124
    statistics 119
    see also Brazil; China; India; Russia;
        South Africa
BRICS Bank 123
Bridge, Gavin 24, 50
bullion banks 58, 59, 62
BullionStar 59
Bush, George H. W. 70

California Gold Rush (1849) 19, 73
Calvão, Filipe 108
Campbell, Bonnie 80
Canada
    Barrick Gold 27, 70, 71, 130
    Bre-X Minerals 66–76
    Chinese mining operations 27
    Klondike Gold Rush (1896–9) 19
    prospectors 45–7
    regulatory failures 74–5
    stock exchanges 51, 69, 72, 75, 130
capital markets 49, 76
    gold standard 19–21
certification 87, 91, 109–11
    Fairtrade 94–6, 109
Chain of Custody Standard 92, 110
Chang Shan Hao Mine 130

Chicago Mercantile Exchange (CME
    Group) 107, 117
child labour 4, 23, 96
China
    ASGM and 27–8
    Belt and Road Initiative 26, 27, 128
    coal-mining companies 26–8
    as development provider 25
    engagement in mining sector 25,
        26–8
    extraction methods 27
    financial sector 131–2
    gold consumption 61, 127–8
    gold investment 120, 131–2, 139
    gold market 128–32
    gold mines in 26, 27
    gold production 26, 52, 125, 127–8
    jewellery 62, 138–9
    mining sector 128–31
    neo-colonialism 25
    new technology 27
    People's Bank of China 120
    see also BRICS
China Gold International Resources
    130
China Gold Investment Bar 132
China National Gold Group
    Corporation (CNGGC) 129–31,
    132
Chr. Michelsen Institute 42
Clapp, Jennifer 114
Collier, Paul 40
Colombia 4
colonial expansion 16–19
    Africa 18
    Latin America 16–17
    neo-colonialism 25
COMEX 117
community development agreements
    (CDAs) 82
conductors 6
conflict
    community-company conflicts 82
    conflict-free supply chains 96–100
    definition of 38

the DRC 100–5
Enough Project 96–7, 101
gold–conflict nexus 38–43
greed model 40
grievance and 31, 37, 40, 50
guerrilla movements 4–5
lootable resources 30, 39–40, 41, 43
social conflict 24
West Africa 38
WGC Conflict-Free Gold Standard
    98–100
conflict resources 38–9
Conteh, Al-Hassan 41
corporate direct targeting 86
corporate social responsibility (CSR)
    81–2, 91
corruption 8, 31
cowboy culture 10, 46, 47, 51, 67, 68,
    144
Crawford, Gordon 28
cross-border smuggling 41, 42–3, 57
cryptocurrency see bitcoin
Cuvelier, Jeroen 104
cyanide 27, 34, 36, 56, 142

da Silva, Genesio Ferreira 1–2, 3
Dauvergne, Peter 85
Dayak people 70, 74
DeBeers 51
decommissioning 55
De Guzman, Michael 68, 69, 72–3
demand for gold 61–6, 113
    China 127–8
    India 127–8
    investment 61, 93–4, 113–17
    jewellery industry 62, 89, 93
    over-the-counter sales 114, 116
Democratic Republic of Congo (DRC)
    Argor-Heraeus SA and 110
    conflict-gold supply chain 101, 102
    Dodd–Frank Act and 100–5
    resource curse 100–1
development providers 25
disclosure regulation 100–5
Dodd–Frank Act 98, 100–5

doré bars 57
Dougherty, Michael 50, 51, 75
Dutch Disease 29

Earthworks 86–7
    No Dirty Gold campaign 87–92
ecological impacts 34–8, 142
    cyanide 27, 34, 36, 56, 142
    environmental damage 27, 34–8
    heap leaching 36, 56
    impact assessments 37–8
    mercury see mercury
    see also environmental damage
Egypt 15–16
Eldorado Gold Corp 131
electronics industry 6, 38, 61, 62
    scrap gold 64
Emergent Technology 107–8
enclave extraction 22–3, 24, 83
    exclusionary spatial enclaves 25
Enough Project 96–7, 101
environmental and social impact
    assessments (ESIAs) 37–8
environmental damage 27, 34–8
    see also ecological impacts
equitable redistribution 33
Erdoğan, Recep Tayyip 154n8
exploration
    financing 50–1
    junior mining companies 49–51

factionalism 32, 33
Fairtrade
    certification 94–6, 109
    Standard for Gold 95, 109
Felderhof, John 68–9, 73–4
Ferdinand of Spain 17
Ferguson, James 22, 25
financialisation 113–17, 143
foreign direct investment (FDI) 22, 80
Fort Knox 60
Fortson, Danny 60–1
fraud
    Bre-X Minerals 66–76
    salting 72–3

Freeport McMoRan Copper & Gold
    Inc. 71, 72
Frobisher, Martin 73

Gallagher, Kevin 25
Geenen, Sarah 104
gender issues 149
German Institute of Global and Area
    Studies 25
Ghana 16, 18
    Chinese mining operations 28
    factionalism 32
    Minerals Development Fund (MDF)
        32–3
    revenue sharing 32–3
    traditional authorities (chiefs) 33
Giuliani, Rudy 154n8
global financial crisis (GFC) 2007–8
    113, 119–20, 123
    gold prices 4, 115
global gold mine production 52, 53
gold
    conductance 6
    continued relevance 3–5
    continuing allure 6–8, 74, 75, 145
    as counter-cyclical 113, 121
    creation of 47–8
    fungibility 6, 7, 58, 107
    future of 144–5
    high value-to-weight ratio 29, 30
    history of 15–16
    investment in see investment in gold
    origins 47–8
    prices see price of gold
    river gold 69, 73
    symbolism 7
    uses 6
Gold Jewelry Corporation Ltd 130
Gold Reserve Act 1934 117
gold reserves
    Australia 126
    Brazil 127
    China 120
    emerging markets 22
    Netherlands 126

Russia 117–18, 125–6
South Africa 126, 127
top ten countries 125
worldwide distribution 52, 53
gold rushes
    Africa 18
    the Amazon 1–2, 3–4, 44, 127
    America 19
    Australia 19
    Bre-X Minerals 66–76
    California 19, 73
    Canada 19
    colonial expansion 16–19
    Fairtrade standard and 96
    recent scramble for gold 21–5, 143–4
    salting and 73
gold standard 3, 19–21
Golden Rules 89, 92
governance see regulation
gradualism 122
Great Depression 20
grievance 31, 37, 40, 50
Gronwald, Victoria 108
growth poles 24
guerrilla movements 4–5
Guinea 43
Gulf Wars 38

Hasan, Mohamad 'Bob' 71
heap leaching 36, 56
Heller, Thomas 29–30
Hilson, Gavin 32–3, 34, 43
Hoeffler, Anke 40
Human Rights Watch 137
Hume, David 20
Humphreys, Macartan 39

Ichikowitz, Ivor 124
impact assessments 37–8
India
    banks 137
    demographics 133, 134
    demonetisation 135
    economic growth 133
    financial system 136–7

gold as collateral 7, 137
gold consumption 61, 127–8
Gold Deposit Scheme 136
gold market 132–7
gold production 132
  investment 136
  jewellery market 62, 133, 134–6,
    137–9
  monetisation 136
  uniform sales tax (GST) 135
  weddings 132
  see also BRICS
Indonesia, Bre-X Minerals 66–76
industry groups 91, 168n17
Initiative for Responsible Mining
  Assurance (IRMA) 85, 92
International Bank for Reconstruction
  and Development 82–3
International Development Association
  82–3
International Labour Organization 96
International Social and Environmental
  Accreditation and Labelling
  Alliance (ISEAL) 91–2
investment in gold 61, 93–4, 113–17
  China 131–2, 139
  gold as counter-cyclical 113, 121
  gold prices and 120–1
  India 136
  over-the-counter sales 114, 116
Iran 5
Ivanhoe Mines 130

Japan 58
jewellery
  China 62, 138–9
  CSR statements 91
  end-use consumer demand 62, 89,
    93
  Enough Project 97
  Golden Rules 89, 92
  India 62, 133, 134–6, 137–9
  No Dirty Gold campaign 86–92
  Responsible Jewellery Council 62,
    91–2, 109–10

scrap/recycled gold 64
supply chain 61–4
Jinfeng Gold Mine 131
Jinhangjia 132
Jinshan Gold Mines Inc. 130
junior mining companies 49–50

Kalyan 137, 138
Kazakhstan 27, 117, 120
Khemka, Nand 124
Kimberley Process Certification Scheme
  87
Kindleberger, Charles 20
Klondike Gold Rush (1896–9) 19
Kluchevskoye Gold Mining Project
  118–19, 123–4
Korten, David 79

large-scale gold mining (LSGM) 24, 51,
  52, 54–7
  government bias 36
  lifecycle 55–6
Latin America
  Chinese mining operations 25, 26
  colonial expansion 16–17
  see also the Amazon
Le Billon, Philippe 39
loans, gold as collateral 7, 137
London
  OTC market 116
  as trading hub 60, 124–5
London Bullion Market Association 58,
  106, 116
London Good Delivery bar 58
lootable resources 30, 39–40, 41, 43

Maconachie, Roy 43, 147
Maduro, Nicolas 5
Mali 16, 24, 41–3
  Bamako 42, 43, 57
  cross-border smuggling 41–2, 57
  export system 42–3
  lax regulation 41–3
  traceability 42
Maloney, Suzanne 5

Marikana massacre 85–6
Matejova, Miriam 85
Mehta, Rajesh 135
mercantilism 17–18
mercury 27, 34, 56, 142
    ecological impact 34–6
    health effects 35
    Minamata Convention 35–6
    national action plans (NAPs) 35
Metalor 58, 59
Minamata Convention 35–6
mine development stage 51–6
mine operation stage 56–7
mine reclamation 55
MKS Finance 110
Mobutu Sese Seko 100–1
Modi, Narendra 134–5, 136
Moody, Roger 82–3
Mulroney, Brian 70
multiplier effects 24
Mun, Thomas 18
Munk, Peter 70

NASDAQ 74
near-field communication chip (NFC
    chip) 106–7
neo-colonialism 25
neo-liberalism 24, 80–1, 82, 123
Netherlands 126
New Development Bank (BRICS Bank)
    123
New York Federal Reserve 60
Nixon, Richard 21
No Dirty Gold campaign 86–92
    Golden Rules 89, 92
non-governmental organisations
    (NGOs) 85
    Earthworks 86–8
NTR Metals 4, 106
NYMEX 117

OECD Due Diligence Guidance 98,
    101, 103
O'Neill, Jim 119, 124
Ontario Securities Commission 74

Ontario Teachers' Pension Fund 74
operation stage 56–7
over-the-counter sales 114, 116
Oxfam America 87

Parker, Stefan 85
Partnership Africa Canada 42
Paxos 107
Pegg, Scott 30
pension funds 8, 74, 116
People's Bank of China 120
Persson, Torgny 58–9
pollution see environmental damage
post-Washington consensus 123
Prevost, Gary 17
price of gold 4, 22, 125, 132
    GFC 2007–8 and 4, 115
    investment in gold and 120–1
    recycling and 64, 115
price–specie flow model 20
privatisation of social services 24, 80–1
Produits Artistiques Métaux Précieux
    (PAMP) 18, 58, 110
public–private partnerships 118

quick response code (QR code) 106–7

'race to the bottom' 36, 79
radio-frequency identification tag (RFID
    tag) 106–7
Rainforest Action Network 169n23
Rajesh Exports 135–6
recycled gold/scrap gold 10, 42, 48, 64,
    93, 115
refineries/refining 57–9, 110, 135
regulation 10, 143, 150, 151
    ASGM and 34, 40, 41
    blockchain 105–8
    Bre-X fraud 66, 67, 74–6
    Canada 74–5
    certification 87, 91, 94–6, 109–11
    Chain of Custody Standard 92, 110
    civil society 84–6
    community development agreements
        (CDAs) 82

competitive deregulation 36, 79
disclosure regulation 100–5
Dodd–Frank Act 98, 100–5
environmental and social impact
    assessments (ESIAs) 37–8
foreign direct investment and 80
home governments 79–80
host governments 79–80
international organisations 82–4
Mali 41–3
misuse of 37
private sector 84–6
'race to the bottom' 36, 79
social relations and 76–7
states 79–82
'track and trace' technology 105–8
see also activists
resource curse 22, 25, 28–31, 101
resource nationalism 81
Responsible Business Alliance (RBA)
    97–8
Responsible Gold 108
Responsible Jewellery Council (RJC)
    62, 91–2, 109–10
Chain of Custody Standard 92, 110
revenue sharing, at local level 31–3
Rio Tinto 51, 56, 110
river gold 69, 73
Rolex 89, 138
Romans 16
Ross, Michael 30, 39
Rosser, Andrew 30–1
Rostow, Walter 29
Royal Mint Gold 107
Russia
    gold production 118, 125
    gold reserves 117–18, 125–6
    Kluchevskoye Gold Mining Project
        118–19, 123–4
    see also BRICS

Sachs, Jeffrey 29
salting 72–3
scrap gold/recycled gold 10, 42, 48, 64,
    93, 115

Seay, Laura 105
'The Sentry' 97
Serra Pelada mine 1–2
shadow state economies 41
shame campaigns 86
Shandong Gold 27, 130
Shanghai Futures Exchange (SHFE)
    117, 131, 132
Shanghai Gold Exchange (SGE) 62,
    117, 131–2
Shanghai Gold Price benchmark 132
Sheth, Chirag 135
SHUBH Jewellers 135
Shvetsov, Sergey 124–5
Sierra Leone 38, 43, 147–9
    women 148–9
Silberfein, Marilyn 41
Simmons, Beth 20–1
Sino Gold Mining Ltd 130–1
smartphones 6
smelting stage 56–7
social relations 47, 76–7, 145
social services, privatisation of 24, 80–1
South Africa
    Chinese mining operations 131
    founding of 18
    gold extraction 26
    gold production 127
    gold reserves 126, 127
    Marikana massacre 85–6
    refining 58
    Second Boer War 18
    Witwatersrand 18
    see also BRICS
South African Gold Fields Ltd 131
specie
    acquisition of 17–18, 139
    price–specie flow model 20
Spiegel, Samuel 35
Standing, André 32–3
storage 59–61
Strathcona Mineral Services 72, 74
sub-Saharan Africa 27–8, 80, 97
Suharto, President of Indonesia, and
    family 70–1, 74

SUN Gold Ltd 124
supply chains 47–66
    blockchain 105–8
    Chain of Custody Standard 92, 110
    conflict-free 96–100
    conflict resources 38
    demand for gold 61–6
    Dodd–Frank Act 98, 100–5
    downstream 61–6
    DRC conflict gold 101, 102
    exploration stage 49–51
    jewellery industry 61–4
    junior mining companies 49–51
    midstream 57–61
    mine development stage 51–6
    operation stage 56–7
    pre-financing 42
    recycled gold/scrap gold 10, 42, 48,
        64, 93, 115
    refining stage 57–9
    regulation see regulation
    smelting stage 56–7
    traceability agenda 96–100
    transportation and storage 59–61
    upstream 48–57
Sustainable Development Goals (SDGs)
    14, 146–9
sweatshops 169n23
Switzerland
    refineries 58, 110, 135
    as trading hub 124–5

Tanaka 58, 59
Tanishq 137–8
taxation 30, 43, 81, 135
TBZ Ltd 137, 138
Tiffany & Co. 89
Toronto Stock Exchange (TSX) 51, 69,
    72, 74, 75, 130
traceability 96–100
    blockchain 105–8
    Conflict-Free Gold Standard 98–100
    Enough Project 96–7, 101
    'first mile' problem 108
    over-the-counter sales 116

Responsible Business Alliance (RBA)
    97–8
    track and trace technology 105–8
trade balances 17–18
    gold standard 20
TransAfrica Capital 124
transparency
    certification and 111
    downstream end of supply chain 61
    Ghana 32, 33
    host institutions 31
    India 133
    refining stage 57
    sampling procedures 73
    transportation 57, 59
trickle-down 25
Trump, Donald 104–5, 154n8
Trustchain 108
TSX Venture Exchange (TSXV) 51, 75
Turkey 5, 61, 117, 120
Tutankhamun's tomb 16
Twain, Mark 46

UK Royal Mint 107
unions 85–6
United Arab Emirates (UAE) 42, 57
United Nations
    Development Programme (UNDP) 14
    Minamata Convention 35–6
    SDGs 14, 146–9
    Security Council (UNSC) 121
United States Bullion Depository 60

Valcambi 58, 135
Vale S.A. 126
Valerio, Greg 99–100
Vanden, Harry E. 17
Veladero mine 27
Venezuela 4, 5
Verisk Maplecroft 81
Victoria Gold Rush (1851) 19
Voyager spacecraft 7

Walsh, David 67–8, 69, 71–2, 73–4
Warner, Andrew 29

Westphalian system 17
Williams, Chad 70
Wolfensohn, James 83
women
  in ASGM sector 23, 96, 148–9
  Sierra Leone 148–9
World Bank 40, 104
  extractive industries review (EIR) 83–4
  grants 82–3
  neo-liberal agenda 82

World Gold Council (WGC) 64, 98,
  113, 114, 132, 137, 141
  Conflict-Free Gold Standard
  98–100

Yamana Gold 108

Zarrab, Reza 154n8
Zhongi Gold 129
Zijin Mining Group 130